I0761920

SLEEPLESS NIGHTS SCRIBBLING

Cover illustration and design by Arjun Unnikrishnan

SLEEPLESS NIGHTS SCRIBBLING

TABLE OF CONTENTS

Foreword

I have been writing on and off since I was 13. It was during the early weeks of my second year of my five years at Jawahar Navodaya Vidyalaya, Idukki that I first started writing. During the tail end of the previous year, one of the seniors in our dorms had told an enthralled audience of a handful of us younger residents a riveting story about a little wizard boy named Harry Potter who went to a boarding school like us, except magical, and that had sparked in me the desire to read the first book in the series. I was immediately hooked. Once I had finished however, I was at a loss to find something else to read because I was at home with access to no books. So I picked up a Malayalam translation of ‘David Copperfield' from a tiny one-room “library” near where I lived, and read it with ample delight. When I came back to school, I had already caught the bug that infects most of us who pick up a good book. I had to write. And I did. I wrote a whole story, in a 200-page lined notebook we used for school and snuck it under the door of the Principal, because he was fond of the talents of his students. The story I had written was of course a pale imitation of Harry Potter, but the kind man read it and invited me up on stage at the school assembly a few days later and gave me a special certificate for my efforts. I was overwhelmed and overjoyed. I promised myself I would be an accomplished writer worthy of this early show of support from someone I respected.

In the two decades since, I haven't kept myself dedicated to that promise I made. Sure, I wrote more in the immediate months after that incident. I managed to write a few hundred pages of a story, the same story I had submitted earlier but divorced from its relation to the more famous boy wizard and situated in my own imagination this time, but lost the manuscript and shortly after, my way as well. Life intervened. The real world called, and she didn't allow for much opportunity to write, or so I kept telling myself over the years. There were bouts of depression. There were romantic escapades, puberty and the confusions of growing up. Education took over. Entertainment took over. Excuses took over. I had ideas. Grand designs, worlds filled with characters that felt real and delightful and menacing and worthy of being brought to life, but I couldn't put pen to paper. I would start a chapter, lose interest or faith in my own skill and it would be tossed. I detoured to research. I decided if I fleshed out my ideas more thoroughly writing would be easier. I collected information, images, references and inspiration like an overzealous magpie. My friends heard my ideas and were curious. I spoke for hours on end to them about the characters, the places, the ideas, the inspirations and they all asked to see what I had written so they could experience it, but there was nothing to give them. I lost confidence, and then interest. I told myself I couldn't write anything. I wasn't a writer, but a wannabe with delusions of grandeur.

Yet over the years the urge to write would sometimes overtake me, envelop me so much that I would be almost compelled to write short pieces. Sometimes it would be in response to a particularly vivid experience I had had, other times it would be some piece of news that forced me to think, and put pen to paper to express what was bubbling up inside me. In time, as life kept pushing the possibilities of writing further and further away, these short bursts became oases that sustained the writer in me. He may have been starved and lonely, but he lived.

Now, I have decided that I should finally take action. In the last few months I have been reinvigorated as life has settled into a pleasant familiarity and a sense of calm has been established. I have been reading more and more, and with that the writer lost in the oases has been seeing it grow and flourish into deeper and more well-watered woods with the rains of inspiration and energy pouring in stronger and more frequently than ever before. I am at a place now where I feel that I should not hide what I have written over the years but share them with people who may have had similar experiences to me as struggling writers.

Every little bit counts. Every time one writes, it is an accomplishment in itself. As I prepare myself to finish two books that I have been writing in recent weeks, I felt that this collection of my writings over the last decade and a half should not be relegated to the shadows any longer. These are short pieces, written as Wordsworth once said in moments where there is "spontaneous overflow of powerful feelings". There is a rawness in them that I can't replicate now, and they are time capsules of me as a writer and as a person. While I am always hopeful that the emotions that reside in them are echoed in others, I hope that in the absence of such at the reader will at least find something that interests them, or sparks feelings in them big or small. There are pieces here that are specific to a certain time and place, especially to Kerala in the 2010s, but there are also pieces that discuss the larger experience of Indians in changing times through my own experiences living through these volatile and interesting decades. I hope this time capsule offers some amount of interest to anyone picking it up.

Writing them has given me flashes of joy and satisfaction in times that have been occasionally desperate and dark, but I can look back on them as building blocks of the person I have become today. I also hope that others like me who may have their doubts regarding their own writing take courage and find the tools to keep that flame alive and thriving. Every small drop of oil is worthwhile if that lamp stays lit as long as one lives and warms one's soul.

I have separated the book into two sections. The first is devoted to short stories, sometimes based on real events, that were written in short bursts of deep feeling that could not be pushed away. The second section includes essays that are longer, discussing specific topics that I felt at various points of time over the years that needed to be addressed as a response to political, social or personal events. I hope the reader finds something worthwhile in each piece to take away, even if in disagreement.

To Amma and Aswathy ma'am.

SHORT STORIES

11

The Sun, a River and a Walk

2014

The sun beat down harshly upon his skin. Sweat formed on his brow, beads slowly inching their way down his face and vanishing into the lush foliage on his chin. A bus raced past him, dust and smoke consuming him in its wake. The bridge was busy as usual, vehicles racing past without the slightest bother of the steady stream of people on either side. He raised his right palm above his face, trying to shield it from the merciless onslaught from the sun above. Eyes squinting, he could barely see where he was stepping, but he knew the road well enough that his feet took him where he wanted to go.

The river had swollen since the last time he had come this way. No doubt, the retreating monsoons had replenished its parched mouth up north. It had rained intermittently for the last few days, but clearly it hadn't been enough to bring the river to its full, once formidable glory. The Bharathapuzha, once a voluptuous beauty in her youth, had grown emaciated after the repeated and unceasing assaults from men dredging up the sand illegally. She was no longer rushing down, tumbling and rolling, but languidly making her way between the numerous sand banks littered across her way. Patches of grass as high as a man grew on either sides of her, and even on the islets dotting her body, and noisy herons fought with the crows for the spoils she left from whatever treasures she bore downriver.

With brisk steps, he climbed off the road and into the sandy path that led down to the shores of the river. In the evenings, it wasn't unusual to find a handful of people just walking along the riverside, enjoying the sunset. The banyan tree, which marked the place where he could cross through the grasses onto the sand, stood as busy with activity as it always did. Birds seemed to think of it as a sin if they passed over it without leaving something behind. The tree looked no longer green, but was a kaleidoscope of whites, greys and browns from months, perhaps years, of aerial carpet bombing campaigns with excrements. The stench was unbearable, the cacophony insufferable. Today, he saw two cages of chicks sitting on the plinth that encircled the tree. The seller might be taking a dip in the river, he thought. Hawking tiny yellow fur-balls like these must be taxing, adorable as they were noisy. He walked on after a cursory peek inside the cages. A few of the chicks seemed dead.

The sand spread out on both sides under his feet. The sun was sweltering, the sand scalding. He liked it, though. It was good to feel the heat on his skin rather than the burning inside, for a change. He looked over the river. The sun was coming down, almost touching the river which had turned into molten gold. He saw a coal black cormorant dive into the river, and was suddenly reminded of Gollum's end. There were people on the ghat. They were the north-Indian labourers who lived around here, he guessed from their looks. Their skin was tan, the kind of rich brown that only came with hard labour and sweating in the sun. Their lithe bodies, naturally toned and taut, spoke of the hours they spent everyday lifting, moving and digging.

One particularly lithe figure was wading out into the river, delicately bracing against the flow. He dipped, moving his strong hands repeatedly over his head to thoroughly drench his hair, and rose with a joyful gasp. There was something childish about the glee on his face, every line wiped clean of the worries and bothers of the day. Water dripped down from his luscious, overly oiled hair, trickling down his lean torso. As he rose out from the water onto the sandbank, he saw the droplets glittering down the small of the man's back and into the curves underneath the light, murky material around his waist. There was power in those strong arms and long, toned legs. A strange wildness radiated from him, something deeply passionate and hungry. The hands moving over him as he soaped himself were rough and calloused, he guessed, but would feel nice against his own sun-warmed soft skin. The eyes were clear, unmarred with any care for what happens later. They seemed to have reached a stage where worrying had no use. All that mattered was this clear flowing water that washed away all the dirt. The man scrubbed his whole body vigorously with the soap, running over his chest, caressing the deep ridges on his abdomen and moving down to the warm secrets under the cloth. His hands moved deftly between his legs, rubbing his inner thigh and moving quickly to his cheeks, and between. Then, he passed the soap on to the next person and dived into the refreshing waters. When he rose, he had the cloth in his hands, unravelled. He twisted it in those strong hands, squeezing out the water into the clear river. Then, careful as not to drench the cloth again, he rose out from the river and for an instant, stood there as the day he was born, the wind caressing his hard frame.

The boy looked away and walked on. The sun was setting fast. It was time to get back. His room was waiting, cold, dark and lonely. The sun set behind him, sinking under the ripples of the river.

And He Walked

2012

He was walking alone. It was a dark, damp night with pregnant clouds sabotaging the crescent moon's attempts to shine through. Beyoncé was singing full-throttle in his ears as he walked along the edge of the nearly deserted road. A few vehicles raced past him now and then. As he went past a grocery store, he noticed the looks of the men chatting as they stood lazily there. He was used to the sight of these prudes staring at his deeply curly, uncut hair and his indifference to their judgmental looks.

He was only a little distance from the grocery store when he noticed someone walking beside him. He glanced at the stranger, and noticed that he was mouthing something.

"Sorry, what did you say?" He said, as he pulled out the earphones.

"Where are you going?" The stranger asked.

Meddlesome prudes indeed, he thought.

"For a walk." He answered and smiled. The stranger did not reciprocate.

"Where do you live? Where are you going" He pressed.

"I live over there, by the temple. Just walking." He answered. He felt a bit uneasy.

"Oh you do, do you. And you're just going for a walk at night?" The stranger said. The boy noticed that he looked a bit dishevelled and his eyes were puffy and red. His hands were grasped behind him.

"Yeah, it's not against the law, you know." The boy said, an edge creeping in unintentionally. The man looked livid now. His hands tightened behind him. The boy felt a kind of jolt pass through him, as he noticed a car following them slowly. Definitely fishy, he thought. He glanced around and moved to the direction of a gate behind which he saw a house with light. He cursed himself internally for choosing to go out during the power-cut. . He hoped that there were people there. The stranger suddenly stopped in front of him as the car pulled up beside him. He saw that there were a few men inside the old Indica.

"You're the kid from Perumbavur aren't you?" the man asked, malice etched in his bloodshot eyes. The boy felt the whiff of liquor wafting from the man.

"What? You're mistaken, pal." He tried to sound calm.

"Am I? What's your name?" He asked, staring into the boy's eyes.

"Ajay. You obviously have the wrong guy." the boy said, trying to convey his utter contempt while holding back any sign of fear. He had a feeling that these men were not from around these parts.

"Mhm, and what do you do?"

"Studying. At M.A College here." He said, giving a side-wise glance at the house, hoping that someone would come to check out the scene.

The stranger was still eying him, contemplating something. He glared right back.

Then, one of the men from the car spoke up.

"We've got the wrong kid. Let's go". The stranger backed towards the car, the boy's eyes still firmly on him.

"Sorry kid, we just thought you were someone we were supposed to do-in tonight." He said as he got in the car, revealing a long scimitar that he had been gripping behind his back. His voice was matter-of-fact.

"Ow, well, okay." The boy answered in a toneless voice. The car drove away, the silence and the cool air returning as if to fill a vacuum. He stood there for a few seconds and caught the voice from his earphones, thin and distant.

He turned around, and walked home, eyes focused straight ahead yet unfocused.

Naeem

2019

Naeem got out of the car, waved at the drawn looking gentleman in the car, and quickly crossed the street. The Gentleman looked distressed, and Naeem could see the effort it took for him to stop himself from coming after him, but he knew the Gentleman wouldn't. The gentlemen never did. Some of them were white and pink, like the one in the car right now, others looked a bit like him except they were brown and could speak his tongue; they were from neighbouring India. Right now, Naeem resolutely walked towards the cinema hall, feeling the eyes of the Gentleman on him. The skinny guard at the gate patted him down lightly, and let him in.

The cinema was dark, but he could make out shapes here and there as the light from the screen danced across the mostly vacant seats. There usually wasn't much movement in here. The figures inside were huddled up in their seats most often, their veins pulsing with the rush of intoxication. Naeem had already found the dealer he trusted, and stalked over to him. They didn't have to speak. The transaction was routine now. Naeem had money this time, so he could dictate the terms. The transaction was quick. He moved back up the aisle, found himself a comfortable seat where the shadows lay thicker, and finally relaxed as the itch that had been growing inside him, his body, was cast away by his rushing blood fed by his purchase.

The Gentleman sat thoughtfully in the car, as it wound its way through the dirty streets of Peshawar back to his hotel. Naeem's words were still ringing in his ears. When he had been with the social worker, Naeem had been sincere. He had promised to quit today. One day at a time. Naeem had been so convincing, his thirteen-year-old face set and ready. And yet as they had stopped near the cinema, he had without hesitation stated that he was going in for some hash and glue. He would rather go in here than the other cinema where they played the porn films. At least in this cinema, his favourite movie played, where the good guys won and the bad guys died in the end. The Gentleman felt nauseated. And yet, he had come all this way to hear, to see, to understand. He couldn't meddle. He was an observer, not a messiah. But he couldn't let his thoughts return to the skinny boy with the big brown eyes and windswept face, currently lying insensate under the influence in the cinema.

*

"I'll take you to a place where it all goes down." Naeem said, as they drove away from the cinema. The Gentleman had come back at dusk, as Naeem had requested.

"Do you know such a place?" The Gentleman asked, although he knew the answer well enough.

Naeem didn't have to say anything. His eyes spoke for him.

The place was a notorious, yet busy intersection. Naeem had been there many a time, doing business for himself and accompanying other boys who were fresh. He considered himself something of a veteran in the field. He had been living in the streets since he ran away from home a few years ago. His parents had died, and his elder brother didn't care much for him. Naeem now spent most of his waking hours doing what most other poor children did around here; collecting recyclable trash from around the city and earning a pittance. A lot of the other boys were sent out by families who couldn't afford to send them to schools or even feed them, and most expected beatings if they didn't make a required amount each day. He didn't have to worry about that because he was his own master. The Gentleman provided for some of the boys, in his facility where they could find a few rotis and gruel on good days. But the nights were never guaranteed.

When they reached the place, Naeem told them to park the car a little distance from the curb. He wanted them to have a clear view, but didn't want their presence to deter possible business.

"Are you sure you'll be safe out there?" Naeem saw the genuine concern etched across the Gentleman's face.

"Don't worry, I can take care of myself", He lied, propping a delicate smile on his face.

When he stepped on to the curb, for a moment he felt his heart skip a beat, because it was a little too dark. The street lamp wasn't working, but there was light from the lamp a little ways behind him. He breathed deliberately, trying to calm his nerves. The Gentleman could see him, at least his silhouette clearly, Naeem was sure. Besides, he had a small microphone tucked inside his worn kurta. They could hear his every word, even his breath, he was sure. He leaned against the railing behind him, and looked around. He was already attracting the attention of a few, he could tell. When you had been living in the streets for as long as he had, even the shades of darkness and stillness told stories of their own. He sensed the man coming over before he saw him. Even through the dark, Naeem could see that the man was fair, slight and in his early twenties by the way he held himself.

The Gentleman saw the young man as well, though he couldn't make out the face. He pressed the headphones closer to his ears, ready to take in everything that was to be said.

"Should we go?" The Man said, looking down at the slender shadow beside him.

"Where?" He heard Naeem's delicate, high voice reply.

"Either the car, or the hotel. Your choice." There was a slight tone of urgency in the Man's reedy voice.

The Gentleman saw Naeem stretch out his arms over his head, in a clear attempt to seem bored and tired.

“What do you want?” He said, plainly. There was no colour in his voice at all.

“You know what I want. I want the night. I’ll pay you a thousand for it”. The Man said, moving to stand beside Naeem, leaning against the railing as well.

“What will I do with a thousand?” Naeem sounded annoyed.

“It’s not like I want to do it all night!”, The Man protested lightly. “It looks like you’re hard. Come with me”.

The Gentleman didn’t blink. He was holding his breath, as if somehow they would hear him through his device.

Naeem looked up at the man, full in his face. He saw the hunger. He saw what The Man would do to him, what pleasure he wanted in return for the measly sum he was offering. He almost smiled.

"I am not going to fuck you." The statement was simple. The statement was final. The Gentleman, back in the car, felt a chill pass through him when he heard the utter finality in Naeem's tone. He had the upper hand here. This time.

His first time, Naeem had been on an empty stomach for three days. He had no money on him. The bus depot was always filled with randy bus-drivers, sleeping on the cots laid out by the owners of eateries, where the drivers could sleep and rest between long drives. A lot of boys also hung around the place, hoping for a place to curl up at night. He had been sleeping on one of the unused cots, when four men had grabbed him and thrown him in a car. Three of them were heroin addicts. They took turns driving themselves inside him, sweating and panting like dogs in the street, and had left him. He had bled. He had fainted. He was all of eight years old. The streets were never safe for young boys in Peshawar. The bache baaz were everywhere. It was an open secret, in this repressed world where women were trophies kept locked inside homes. He was always on the lookout since then, and like nearly every other boy he knew, he had found himself drugged, and toyed with by men. They gave him soft drinks. Food. Sometimes they curled up with him after, and gave him warmth through the night, their sweat mingling and dripping down their bodies. And now, when he needed money for the drugs, or for food, or if he wanted to go to the cinema, he knew where and how to get it. If his flesh was for the taking, he could sell it just as well and make something out of it. There were plenty of men around, and he was a pretty boy. That first time, he had cried. Never since.

*

Naeem sat on the chair to The Gentleman's left. Across from him, sat his brother. He looked like a rugged, older version of Naeem, but with none of his prettiness. His eyes were bloodshot, staring across the table at Naeem with unmistakable animosity.

Across from the Gentleman sat a dignified lady, a little past her youth, with her glasses perched on the top of her head. She had flown in from Karachi. She ran a rehabilitation centre there, and wanted to take Naeem with her. She wanted to give him a chance. She had been a silent witness to the conversation going on between the men, taking it all in. The Gentleman had found scars on Naeem's limbs, small cuts on his arms and wrists, but also one that was once clearly a deep gash. He was concerned for Naeem's life. Naeem looked agitated and sweaty, unable to look at the Gentleman. His eyes scanned the room, his brother, and were now fixed on a spot on the table.

"Are you aware that Naeem has been selling himself to men?" the Gentleman asked the Brother.

"He's a dirty little thing. Dirty people do dirty things" He replied, though there were words left unsaid.

"Had he told you when he was raped at the bus depot?"

“Him? No. But that’s his own sin. We’re honourable people, and he’s making us lose honour in the village. In the clan. I would give him such a beating right now, but won’t, only because of you here”, Brother said, his eyes darting between the Gentleman and the Lady. Then he looked at Naeem.

“Will you run away again? Will you run from Karachi and come back here?” His eyes were daggers, his voice ice.

“No, I promise. This time I won’t”. Naeem was a 13-year-old boy, and sounded smaller, cowed.

“Then if you don’t object, he can go to Karachi. Do you agree with that?” The Gentleman asked.

The Brother looked stone-faced at Naeem. There was hatred and anger there. But there was also relief.

“Yes.” He signed the documents placidly, and left.

*

The first week in Karachi, Naeem was kept in a locked room, as he went through withdrawal. And when he was finally let out, a cloud hung over him. He wanted to leave. It was worse than prison here. He couldn't live if he had to stay here for three months. As he was walking towards the doctor's office, his face was gaunt. He knew his fate. They had taken his blood. They had sent it away for testing. He had been raped, and used so many times that he couldn't even count that high. He was terrified now. As long as he had been ignorant, he was safe. Now he had no escape from facing the truth.

He was ready to accept his fate. He had been a sinner. He had let himself be buggered, many times, by many men. He had sought them out. Old men. Young men. Rich men. Druggies. Drivers. And…he had been wicked as well. He had forced himself on a boy. The Boy had agreed to come with him to the movies, and he had bought him a soda. But after the movie, he hadn't wanted to do it. So he had pulled him away and pushed himself inside him. He had done what had been done to him. He couldn't be saved. He didn't deserve to be saved.

He walked into the doctor's office and sat down. His eyes were down, a haunted look in them. Dark shadows lined his face, which spoke plainly of pains beyond his years. The doctor was rifling through paperwork, and Naeem couldn't bring himself to look up. He knew the verdict.

"The results came out clear, *Bache*." He said, kindly. "You are clean."

Naeem didn't react. Had he heard the words right? Had he understood? The doctor smiled paternally at him, looking him in the eyes.

And then the clouds parted. Life seemed to seep back into Naeem's face. A whisper of hope creeped up from somewhere, and suddenly he was a kid again. Naeem smiled, unable to stop himself. He knew what he had to do now. He had to try. That's all he had, a chance. And he would try.

P.S. This piece is based on a documentary regarding the practice of bacha bazi in Pakistan called "*Preying On Young Boys: Pakistan's Hidden Predators*" which is freely available on Youtube. I was struck by the prevalence of the practice and deeply shocked by the rawness depicted in the documentary, and was pushed to write this piece by a very visceral need.

ESSAYS

Finding My Indianness

2014

"Unity in diversity". This tagline has been associated with my understanding of India for as long as I can remember. I was told from childhood that India is a land of rich culture, of varied peoples with unique ideals separate from, and superior to, the rest of the world, living in perfect harmony. I was taught from an early age to think of myself as an Indian - a person who belonged to the list of unnumbered such souls that filled the land from Kanyakumari to Kashmir, Nagaland to Gujarat. I was an Indian, and I should be proud of it. It felt like I was part of a delicious *avial*, if you will; odd and seemingly incongruous ingredients making a delicious final product somehow.

Then I grew up, and went through hours of History, Geography and such wondrous other subjects in school, and realised that India wasn't, as I was lead to believe, a unified and internalised concept for longer than perhaps the last 60-70 years (at least, to its own residents). I learnt of our freedom struggle, how it united the various peoples across the vast subcontinent regardless of age, gender, religion, station and cast. I learnt of the age of kings before, of the Mughals and the Mauryas, the Rajputs and Cheras and the numerous other dynasties that came before and established their strongholds across the country. I came to know about the coming of the muslim invaders from the northwest and the arrival of Islam, and the bringing of Christianity through the southern coast and its influence on the natives. The birth of Mahavira and Sidhartha Gautama and the impact of their ideals and spread of their respective followers were taught to me, and so were the legends of Rama and Krishna and the tales of the great epics. And in all this confusing méleé, I realised that there never was a clearly defined nation called India. If there was one, it was just a notion of the people belonging to a few communities or to different geographical areas within the Indian subcontinent, and perhaps for the invading armies and other external entities. India was a unified whole in the eyes of the Others that kept on coming to her for whatever reasons throughout the centuries; the trading Others, the travelling Others, the plundering Others and finally, the ruling Others. Only after throwing off the yoke of British imperialism, that 'evil Western' foe of ours that shaped the whole of India's character since, has this modern entity of a united India taken shape as it stands today. It is clear that India, Bharath or Hindustan was more a product of exclusion because of its geographical isolation and historical seclusion rather than any other unifying force from within like most, if not all, nation-states in the world. The people between the Himalayas and the southern ocean were Indian, a single entity, no matter what differences the people living therein had because of a shared connection, often tentative and through shared memories and stories rather than unambiguous political and personal identification. This did nothing to buoy my spirits in finding my Indianness. So apparently, I was Indian because I wasn't Persian, Chinese, or Russian? That simply would not do.

Then I turned my attention to finding what made this nation of 29 states and 7 union territories 'India'. What was it that made me an Indian, aside from the fact that I happened to be born here. What it meant to belong to the Indian community, and the celebrated 'Indian Culture' that was being paraded around by certain individuals and socio-political agencies in order to declare who didn't belong to it. Was it my birth within the political boundaries that made me an Indian? Or was it the fact that I belonged to Hinduism (the ways of life of the people beyond the Sindhu) or Sanatana Dharma, the prominent and original religion (for lack of a better word) of the inhabitants of the Indo-Gangetic plains that defined my Indianness? However, going in that vein would mean that all those people from the other religious denominations here would be excluded as un-Indian, which I knew to be simply stupid. Also, that would mean Hinduism was a monolith that stayed consistent and unchanged throughout time and space, which I also knew not to be true. Therefore, I discarded that approach.

Then I thought that maybe my dark skin, dark hair and dark eyes were a sign of my innate Indianness, because that was what I saw as a common feature among the people I knew around me. But that meant the fair-skinned, or rather "wheat-complexioned" northerners and the mongoloid descendants of the Northeast were not Indian on my scale. Absurd, I know. So I threw that measure out the window. I knew language could never be a measure of Indianness, because India had 22 scheduled languages (to my knowledge) and innumerable dialects. I mean, my mother tongue was Malayalam, and I could not have a real conversation with someone just 150 km to my east, unless I tried using Hindi or English. So unless Hindi, the "northern" language, or English, the language of the "foreigners", were taken as a common denominator, I was screwed out of my Indianness. That was a no-go. Unsurprisingly, I was very disheartened at this point, because I was running out of criteria to justify my Indianness. What was that elusive thing that made me undoubtedly Indian? What was that unifying factor that made not just me and a few other handful, but the whole 1.2 Billion people who called this land their home, unquestionably Indian? I didn't know. I was baffled. I mean, when somebody said 'American', the images that came to my mind were overweight white people in tight t-shirts munching on burgers or barbecuing everything that moved while burning books and shooting guns or scantily–clad girls doing the duckface or crying about being triggered by something, or beer-chugging frat-boys yelling racist slurs. Or the cast of FRIENDS. When thinking of the British, the image of the Queen, Harry Potter and red buses crowded my mind, populated by pale people who spoke either posh English or cockney while eating fish and chips and being politely offended by immigrants. China meant exotic colours, an inscrutable script and sweet, short people with fierce pride in their culture. Japan was a technological haven filled with smart, albeit sex-obsessed, people with technicolour lives. But whenever I thought of India, there never was that single universal image that came to mind. Most times, it was the sights and sounds of Kerala, my first love. There were also the wheat-fields of the north, the distant, almost alien Himalayas, the graceful shapes of Bharatanatyam dancers as well as Madhuri Dixit doing a Bollywood dance. My mother in the temple with the jasmine in her hair was India for me, my friend Annu in her Punjabi salwar too, just as much as the Juma Masjid in Delhi meant India to me. Krishna and Radha were as much Indian to me as two of my guy friends having a tender moment were. All of these often conflicting images were what made my vision of India. Different colours and different shades, each different yet seeping into each other seamlessly.

Nevertheless, lately, I have seen a drastic change in the perception of what an Indian is. There seems to be no more space for pluralism. An Indian 'has' to be a certain way, or so some people would have us believe. Especially in these last few years, I came across many people, including quite a few of my friends and relatives, who were all for "restoring India" and "protecting Indian culture from alien forces of contemptible intentions", though no one seemed particularly bothered to define what they meant by this ominous pronouncement. What I gleaned from all the zealous talk was that they intended to ward off alleged evil Western influences like capitalism, Christianity, Islam, homosexuality, brand culture, pop music etc. and preserve the original Indian culture or something to that effect. It didn't take me long to find the folly of these ideas. What these persons were propagating was a sectarian restrictive version of cultural identity that wasn't Indian at all. In the guise of Hindu principles (apparently because India was after all a Hindu nation after the partition in 1947, in their understanding) the ideas being paraded around were extremely narrow, outdated concepts, in the similar vein the Westboro Baptist Church used the Christian faith to spread their own deluded judgments. True, Hindu culture was indeed one of the more ancient of the many cultures that flourished in the subcontinent, but the fact was it too was an ever-evolving entity, never a constant and stagnant one like it was being labelled. The culture of India as it stands today was undeniably the product of the many internal and external forces that acted upon the people and their lives over the past few thousand years and the many religious and cultural practices that were extant in the subcontinent and adapted to changes around them. The coming of Islam, the varying sultanates in Delhi and the Deccan, the arrival of Vasco da Gama and the other western traders and powers, the spread of Christianity through missionaries in most of India and the first wave of Christianity in Kerala, the numerous invasions by eastern and northwestern tribesmen, the unique geographical and cultural canvas of each part of India; all these ingredients added to the melting pot that was (and is) India to form this most multicultural of societies in the world.

Indian culture, as I see it, is an ever-changing, constantly mutating concept with roots in the ancient Vedic traditions and other religio-philosophical concepts that grew in positive or negative association with it, which simply cannot be defined by any of the conventional parameters. Why so? Because there is no such thing as a unified "Indian Culture" that defines a representative "Indianness" for its multicultural people. It is a set of unique micro-cultures spread across its vast landscape, different from each other in distinct and original ways, yet having certain shared threads that give it a semblance of unity. Because of its unique position; sheltered in the north by one of the most formidable mountain ranges in the world, and the Bay of Bengal, Arabian Sea and Indian Ocean on the east, west and south respectively, the Indian subcontinent has had a rather secluded existence. Sure, many other cultures have come and gone, but none have managed to truly eradicate the native traditions of the landmass, and have instead ingratiated themselves to the original vibrant symphony. It shows the fact that the variety and multiplicity of cultures in India are its greatest asset as a society. It is rich, varied and unique in ways no other culture in the world is, and it is all thanks to the ability of the prevalent customs, traditions and cultures to readily appropriate and adapt foreign elements into it and thus replenish and refurbish its existence. A devout malayali Syrian-Christian is as much an Indian as an atheist bengali who nevertheless celebrates the durga-puja for its cultural value.

As we all know, regional differences and conflicts are more immediate to us than any other potential threat externally. We are all either Tamilians or Marathis or Gujarathis or Christians inside, but evidently the 'Indian' within us all awakes when the threat is external. It is the elusive Other that unites us, that grants us our Indianness. Our religious and cultural canvas is much too varied to be titled as 'Indian' at one go among ourselves. Our culture, in truth, is a smorgasbord of micro-cultures sharing tenuous tendrils as binds, each similar and dissimilar to the one next to it in unique and unpredictable ways. The white

Chatta-Mundu clad nasrani women of Kerala are as Indian as the devout, effervescent Konkani Christians of Goa. But throw in an external Other, like the threat of a war with Pakistan or competition in the global economy with China, then we are suddenly more than the sum of all our partial identities. Otherwise, apart from our passports or aadhar cards, there isn't anything universal that defines even a majority of us in the modern nation of India that defines us as Indian. When someone in Uttar Pradesh has something more in common with a regular person from Lahore, or when a lady from Chennai has more in common with another from northern Sri Lanka that either has with the aforementioned duo, we have to realise that arbitrary notions pushed by politicians do not define our identities.

So why this clamour to 'preserve' a non-existent thing? Is it a fear of change? Is it plain selfishness, an unwillingness to realise the fact that one's ideas and beliefs have become outdated and archaic? I don't know.

What India is, is a multi-cultural potpourri surviving, indeed thriving, because (and not in spite) of its pluralities. It is because of the array of influences, adaptations and assimilations throughout the ages that India is one of the most heterogeneous cultures in the world. It is when homogeneity is forced upon its people; whether linguistic, cultural, religious or racial, that there is discord and disharmony. Negation of its multiplicities is refuting its rich history and identity. Being Indian is all about being many things at once and being fine with it. It is being a Hindu teenager who thinks in English, but speaks Malayalam, wearing a 'Godzilla' T-shirt, while enjoying a meal of spicy Chinese takeout with a Muslim or Christian classmate, who is clad in a traditional churidar and believes that evolution is a myth. It is knowing that the Harappans, the janapadas, the Mauryas, the Guptas, the Cheras, the Cholas, the Hoysalas, the Tuluvas, the imperial Mughals, the Marathas, the Travancorians etc are all part of that process of evolving Indianness, and that fighting about perceived differences and incidents from centuries ago is an exercise in futility only benefitting politicians who want to manipulate people for personal gains alone. That is what Indianness is all about. It means being many things yet transcending them. It is understanding that because we are all different from each other in one way or another while also recognizing how we are connected in a multitude of other ways but being open and accepting of these differences and partaking joyously in the celebrations of these differences.

That is my Indianness.

The Young Hypocritical Indian

2017

"Boys don't have long hair. Boys don't grow their fingernails. Boys don't need chapsticks, or tweezers for their eye-brows. Boys don't wear kajal in their eyes."

These are some of the lines I have dealt with ever since I was little. In a society where masculinity is welcomed and femininity is shunned at a very deep, almost subconscious level, it is no surprise that such comments are nothing new to someone who dabbles in androgyny and refuses to accept social 'norms' of gender. When we are children, dressing up or being 'girly' or 'tom-boyish' can be viewed at best as kids in play, at worst as not knowing any better. But past a certain age, it will become 'rebellious', 'unseemly' and 'ridiculous'. We are all expected to play certain roles in life, regardless of our own choice in the matter. Men are Masculine, women Feminine, and any spillage of one into the other is reproachable, inexcusable and unacceptable. The worst thing a man can be is feminine, or womanly, and the greatest faux pas a woman can commit is overreach and be manly. One has to learn to conform to one's gender, and follow the strict watertight guidelines assigned to them at all times. If anyone dares to try, then they might as well be ready for all the ridicule, criticism and possible harassment aimed at them. Men who show the slightest signs of accepting the femininity in them have their sexuality questioned (because they can't possibly be "real men"), and a woman who shows typical masculine attributes like wearing men's shirts or riding motorbikes are either bossy, or in need of a 'firm hand'.

Looking at the portrayal of men and women in the mass media, we can see how notions of gender are shoved down people's throat from a very young age. Be it in the movies, music, ads ir in print, the images conveyed have always been of the superiority of macho 'cool guys' (much to the detriment of such outcasts as nerds, geeks, effeminate men and those not inclined to sports or alcohol and partying), and of gorgeous women who are after a man of their dreams, or married women who are either happy or unhappy with the men they have. In all my years of prolific television bingeing, I have yet to come across anything that really shatters this mould, and challenges the gender-conformist messages that are planted into our minds. New ideas and new perspectives are extremely few and far between, and rarely make much of an impact in the mainstream or in the minds of the layman. (Notice how it's layMAN, chairMAN, huMAN, HIStory...). It's all an abundance of cloying clichés and tired caricatures masquerading as 'reality'. I also am forced to believe that all the homophobia and transphobia in this country has a lot to do with this belief in the inferiority of the feminine and disregard for the fact that gender is a construct and the realities of people are far from uniform (apart from rampant ignorance, bigotry and plain stupidity, of course.). It has something to do with the fact that sexuality and gender are taboo topics in our oh-so lauded country with the ever-manipulated history, and these non-conformist entities challenge the accepted gender-sexual 'norms' which are believed to be "right" or "natural" (a debatable nomenclature by all means).

In India we enforce these rules vigorously, with the emphasis of and on culture and religion. Sexuality, gender, personal identity, individual notions of spirituality and art - all these topics are almost always absent in the public discourse until and unless it is something 'controversial' or sensational that enables some political or religious group to take advantage of it. With politics becoming more and more influenced by and influential in religion and culture in our country, and it being used as a tool for mass-mobilisation even for petty causes much to the detriment of the actual cultures (yes, plural) of this country, it should come as little surprise that we as a people have become extremely intolerant and incapable of accommodating an outsider perspective. This reflects perfectly in the way we handle anything related to sex, gender and sexuality; be it the KOL episode, the ridiculous Porn Ban or the absolutely insane double-standards when it comes to Sunny Leone (Because of course, we should blame anything else but the actual convicts for rapes and molestations and sexuality violent attitudes). We are ready, willing and able to be lewd and sexual in unnecessary circumstances, but woe befall anyone who has the guts to stand up for their principles and call this out. When women are perceived as property, it is not surprising that marital rape is an a-OK 100% legal thing, but consenting adults of whatever gender having private intimate times is 'public indecency'. And don't even get me started on the incompetent, ignorant bullies and thugs known as the Moral Police, who have hardly any more value (or morals) than that offensive thing left unflushed in a public toilet.

And this is not an age-thing, or among the less literate even. The amount of sheer stupidity and ignorance of today's youth is staggering. How do I know? Because thanks to social media, they are all out there rubbing their ignorance in our faces. Ignorance amongst the lower strata of society without access to proper education (What a joke, 'proper education!) is understandable, though unacceptable. But among the middle class, and those spoiled Richie Rich's with their shiny cars and Ivy-league educations? Now that is just insulting. It seems like they just don't care about anything that doesn't concern them immediately, and are happy to parrot the beliefs fed to them, by their parents, family, religious leaders or misguided teachers who most likely have strong agendas of their own. They never bother to take anything beyond face-value, and rarely try to peruse beyond empty facades. This attitude of indifference is a crippling flaw in an otherwise mostly active generation, and doesn't bode well for the future of this hodgepodge called India.

Now, don't get me wrong. I'm not saying that all the young men and women of our country, so vast and diverse it's a sin to try to think of it in any way homogeneous, are vain, shallow beings without an ounce of social responsibility, personal integrity or interest in the multitudinous cultures of our peoples, but we do seem to have more than our share of them. Times have changed since I was just a young boy who couldn't ask questions or expect answers. I know enough people to know rational discussion and an open mind are readily available at all turns if one just looks in the right places, but the sheer amount of people one deals with, with brains thicker than overcooked rice, is overwhelming. Rooted in their unflinching belief that the ideas preached to them from their cultural idols are absolute, and refuse to listen to reason at all costs, take pleasure in disparaging anyone who doesn't bat for their team and twist facts to achieve their oh-so deluded ends. These men (and women) pride themselves for not being "persuaded" by the "feminist lobby", or adamantly vilify the LGBTQ community as the Antichrist and are quite keen to ostracise and bully anyone who does not buy into their version of history or "truth" (and believe me, their versions are more embellished than the Bible). And thanks to social media they don't have any qualms whatsoever in airing their soiled knickers for all the world to see (and find like-minded deviants, of course). It is, at times, most ironic to see people harp on, waxing (not so) eloquently on the evils of Western influence and culture, of how degraded our own sacred culture has become, how English is the Devil's own infliction upon this good earth and how foreign ideas like feminism, marriage equality, Queer identities and liberal spirituality, all while posting a highly filtered selfie with a duckface in their new Levis using a brand new Iphone, because that is, after all, the epitome of present day Indianness; criticising anyone who doesn’t conform to the “norm” while being oblivious to one's own flaws.

Honour and Other Lies

2018

At one point during the nearly three hour runtime of Sanjay Leela Bhansali's latest entry in the Deepika-Ranveer saga, the titular Padmavati asks her husband Maharawal Ratan Singh permission to perform Jauhar, the act of self-immolation, in the event of his death at the hands of Alauddin Khilji. In the world of Padmavat (erstwhile Padmavati), even death cannot be achieved without the say-so of the husband.

Everyone who hasn't been living under a rock over the last few months is aware of the huge, and unnecessary, hullabaloo surrounding Bhansali's bloated paean to the valour of the Rajputs, Padmaavat, which has created a climate of racial tension and violence in some of the regressive states of Northern India. It tells the story of Rani Padmavati of Mewar, the second wife of Maharawal Ratan Singh, and how she was coveted by Alauddin

Khilji of the Delhi Sultanate because of her beauty, and his urge to collect her leads to a war between the two men and their forces. The Rajputs, as in most other cases in their long celebrated but often rewritten history, inevitably fall and the women are then forced by their regressive traditions to commit jauhar. There's much to unpack in this film, least of all the film itself as a piece of art or entertainment.

The controversy surrounding the film was sparked by extremist Rajput and Hindu outfits objecting to the perceived dishonourable portrayal of their beloved righteous Rani Padmini. Like oh so many other such cases of ignorant people creating chaos in the name of apparent slight to misplaced honour (films like *Haider, Aaja Nachle* and *PK* come to mind) this is blown quite out of proportion, unnecessary and frankly indicative of the backward mindset of the perpetrators and the general unfavourable climate presently extant in India. India, as Amir Khan rightly said (and then had to retract so as not to suffer the unpleasant consequences) is intolerant, and the huge brouhaha about nothing just goes to prove it once again. Besides, what shocks me is the fact that there is no outcry from certain other communities who actually are at the receiving end of the calculated malicious portrayal.

The plot of the film is based on the 16th century poem by Sufi poet Malik Muhammed Jayasi (Jaisi) and predominantly deals with Rajput honour in the face of threat from a mightier foe. In the wake of this firestorm, the most ridiculous thing is that there is no historical figure that equates to the (in)famous Rani Padmini. While Alauddin Khilji and Ratan Sen are real historical figures from the 14th century, and Khilji did attack and conquer Chittor without hassle, there is no evidence of any Rani Padmini in any historical records of the time or since. The character of Padmini/Padmavati was birthed by the imagination of the poet Jayasi, for his fictional allegorical epic poem that happened to make use of real historical figures 200 years after the fall of Chittor. It was the later Rajput poets and bards, upon the patronage of various Rajput priests, who added and embellished the original tale with sprinklings of Rajput valour and honour to curry favour and sway contemporary society. The fact remains that based on contemporary historical evidence and extensive studies of periods thereafter, the tale of Padmavati is a myth that has been erroneously peddled as a version (an alternative fact, in today's parlance) by the Rajputs (most likely to save face, as is the case with most losers in wars). It is among a long list of such fictional alternative histories prevalent in India that is central to the Hindutva school of thought, which cannot seem to separate myth and allegory from history and fact. So for starters, the very cause for which the Karni Sena and other indigenous terrorists are so incensed about is based on falsities, all smoke and mirrors.

As for the film itself, I went into the cinema without much expectations, intent on reserving judgement until fully immersing myself in this cinematic experience as offered by the most grandiose filmmaker in Bollywood. After the spectacle-laden overkills of *Ram-Leela* and

Bajiraao Mastani, we know what to expect from an SLB production, and the film most definitely delivers in most ways. The film seems more like the third entry in a franchise that includes the two previous Bhansali films, because one could easily recut all three films together and make a cohesive single film. The visual palette is almost identical; reds and oranges are awash in nearly every frame, weird contact lenses are a dime-a-dozen. Even the music is cut from the same cloth, sounding more like retreads of the same 3-4 songs from the days of *Hum Dil De Chuke Sanam*; there's the *Dhol Baaje*-type dance number for the heroine (complete with watered down Classical Dance 101 steps and dime-store Madhuri Dixit expressions and voluminous skirts) and the *Laal Ishq* number, the same melody sung by a plaintive male voice to evoke the same feeling of pathos, ubiquitous to all four of his non-*Devdas* romances, *Hum Dil De Chuke Sanam, Ram-Leela, Baajirao Mastani* and now this.

At close to three hours, the film is long and exhausting, saved mostly by the visuals on display. Bhansali is best at creating incredible spectacles, and there's more than enough of that in spades. Apart from the unnecessary addition of tacked-on 3D, the visuals are predictably lush and rich, impeccable and grandiloquent, and far better than the previous pairings of Ranveer and Deepika. But it borders on being garish, assaulting the senses with unnerving grandeur and opulence. Every frame is beautifully captured, and the Bhansali flair for framing the scenes as beautifully as possible is at full-throttle, but just like its predecessors, the film values spectacle over substance, overridden with clichés and unsubtle storytelling. No matter how pretty the package, the content is flimsy at best. The acting is consistently good, and reliable, bordering on great, but the actors can't simply rise above the trite material they are dealing with. Deepika Padukone looks absolutely stunning, the best she has ever looked on film (capturing the beauty of his principally young cast is probably Bhansali's biggest achievement). But she yet again relies on the same bag of tricks she has pulled out on her other tragic romances, making her way through the same four faces she has deployed since her time on *Om Shanti Om*; her trump card is that "tear-in the eye-gritty-smile-and-resolve" combo that is present in all her big romances. Shahid Kapoor looks resplendent, but his character is such a cliché, and so blandly played, one can't help but feel sorry for the talent behind such gems as *Haider*. Aditi Rao Hydari is subtle and nuanced in her performance, beautiful and poised, but yet again the character of Mehrunisa is far too flimsy to carry much weight. Much of the heavy-lifting is done by Ranveer Singh. Much like the hunks of meat he devours throughout the film (blatantly exploiting the crude "Maasahari Muslim" cliché) he dives into each moment on screen with utmost relish. His acting is very much in the post-*All About Eve* Bette Davis School of scene-chewing. Each word is delivered with such sheer gusto and with the most amount of artifice possible; he's practically devouring everyone else in the scene. One is reminded of singers like Mariah Carey and Christina Aguilera who never let a chance go to cram 700 notes in one syllable when just 4 would do, and this is the acting equivalent of the same. No doubt, award-baiting, an unabashed urge to join the ranks of such iconic movie villains as the Joker, Scar and Darth Vader is behind this over-the-top and at times grotesque portrayal that borders on caricature.

The issues of the film though, are not significantly in its presentation, but reside in its underlying themes, content and intent. The film begins with a bevy of disclaimers, every single one it can throw at the audience, forewarning its fictional nature and no doubt stemming from its troubled and controversial production and rollout. The story itself, and the way Bhansali and co. handle the subject is problematic. The film is incredibly opportunistic in this climate of religious fanaticism, political manoeuvring and the growing unpleasantness between the Hindutva brand and everybody else. The film panders to the sensibilities of the kind of reactionary Hindu who subscribes to this school of Hinduism that takes everything at face-value and considers anything not aligned to their version of Indian culture (as misguided and misinformed it may be) as a contemptible Other that has to be taken down. The blatant glorification of Rajputana is sickening to behold. The film celebrates archaic traditions which are absolutely outdated, chauvinistic and entrenched in patriarchal stereotypes. The obvious goal of the film is the elevation of an idealised Rajput culture (standing in for the majority Hindu culture, at its glorified best) and vilify the Delhi Sultanate, and by extension the whole of Muslim monarchy in India. Regardless of historical accuracy or validity, they are constantly separated as a distinct outsider, and the period before it being celebrated as the Golden Age of India, discounting every major accomplishment of the Sultanate and the Mughals and their many gifts to Indian society and history. In Padmavat, the two male monarchs quickly establish this dichotomy. Ratan Singh is the ever-handsome, virtuous and righteous Hindu king, his kingdom rich and opulent, serene and serendipitous. On the other end, the Khiljis are forever shrouded in the dark and dank, their clothes and general appearance quite shabby and crass, their practices depicted as barbaric and animalistic. The ideal pure-vegetarian Ratan Singh nibbles dainty morsels from exquisite *thaalis* in the open air, the gluttonous and ravenous Khiljis gorging on huge limbs, tearing chunks of meat right off the bone like the Dothraki (who are clearly the inspiration for the Khiljis here). Ratan Singh is always polished and in control, Alauddin chaotic and wild. Even when Ratan Singh ditches his first wife for no apparent reason and marries Padmavati from the distant Singhala, that is a celebration of her beauty and love; meanwhile the despicable Alauddin is a debauched pervert who humps a serving girl on his wedding day, and even has a homosexual servant Malik Kafur who carries out all his twisted needs. (GASP!!)

The glorification of the Rajputs and the demonization of Alauddin Khilji drives the plot, but even the simplest introspection reveals the flimsy base upon which this house of cards is built. In this film celebrating Rajput honour and valour, the inevitable fall of Chittor is unquestionably the fault of the Rajputs themselves and their faulty decisions throughout the narrative. Despite the much praised lyonization of the Rajputs, Chittor falls due to the unwarranted pride of its men, the cowardice and disunity amongst the Rajput clans and the many flaws in their tactics; the king literally walks into a trap. Tellingly, no other Rajput king comes to aid Chittor so as not to antagonise the Sultan of Delhi. The glorified embodiment of the stereotypical Hindu ruler is typified by these Rajputs of Chittor, who stumble from one blunder to the next against a vastly superior foe who is at once much more developed militarily and economically and yet is depicted as the stereotypical savage force of a traitorous Muslim empire. The innately chauvinistic nature of the Rajputs is dusted under the carpets, though. Even when trying to depict the story of a powerful feminist royal who hunts, rides and is intelligent, her life is spent as the obedient wife to a prideful fool and then ends in a war where she is just an accessory. Though far more intelligent in tactics and maneuvering politically than the men around her, Padmavati has no option but to commit suicide along with every other woman in the castle (in one especially sickening shot, we see a terrified young girl and a pregnant woman racing towards the pyre) because of course women have no agency over their own lives or bodies and the honour of their sometimes idiotic men is paramount. The failure of the Chittor Rajputs is, as mentioned earlier, in their own foolhardy actions, from not taking the threat of Khilji seriously, celebrating Diwali and Holi while under a siege, having prepared no warnings for the coming of an attack from the greatest military and economic power of the age, then basically repeating statements of Rajput valour without actually doing anything about the immense and replenishable army camped outside, the king walking into incarceration, sacrificing 800 able men only to have the escape of the king possible because of Alauddin's own wife, and then facing Alauddin in single-combat while his whole army and ample resources are at hand to easily take over the diminished and demoralised army of Chittor. The ineptitude and traditions disguised behind "Valour" and "Honour" seem downright foolish especially when they seem to know the opposition to be treacherous and cunning. The double standard is almost laughable, with the vastly superior and advanced Sultanate depicted as barbaric, and the Rajput with two wives looking down on the effeminate "begum" Malik Kafur of his foe who is stated to be lecherous and uncouth. The innate islamophobia and homophobia is as unsubtle as Ranveer's own overtly homoerotic (yet PG-13) portrayal of the evidently giant personality of Alauddin Khilji. It is laughable, these blatant attempts at maligning the two, because Alauddin Khilji WAS the Sultan of India, and Malik Kafur was his right hand (possibly his lover as well), and was a far better warrior than the Chittor Rajputs seeing as he managed to repel Mongol invasions and defeat the Yadavas, Kakatiyas, Hoysalas and the Pandyas. There is also the hypocrisy of Bhansali in his apparent homophobia, whose films have always been unabashedly homoerotic and queer-baiting, what with the lingering near-naked shots plentiful of his young nubile male leads (Salman in HDDCS, Ranbir in *Saawariya*, Ranveer in *Ram-Leela* and *Baajirao Mastani*, and Shahid in this one). In fact, throughout the film, the only three people who seem to operate on any kind of logic are the three primary non-Rajputs; Alauddin, Padmavati and Mehrunisa.

The blatant opportunistic islamophobia of the film is the most irksome factor about the whole enterprise (apart from that other disturbing thing we will discuss later) particularly as it is based on a long tradition of portraying the "Muslim era" of Indian history as a rule of outsiders and traitorous savages. This Othering of anyone, particularly Muslims, in the country's long history is nothing new, but it is extremely reprehensible and frankly unfair. The very basic concept of Hinduism was inclusiveness and assimilation, but apparently these new "Hindus" don't know Hinduism at all. Reliable history contradicts the popular and populist representation of such figures and Alauddin Khilji, as is in this film and perpetrated by the Hindutvawadis. The self-worshipping and cocky Rajputs and their often foolhardy actions have historically almost always ended in their defeat and humiliation, with no prominent Rajput king having successfully defeated any of the major Sultans of Delhi or the Mughals. In the actual, verifiable history of northern India the conflicts between the warlike Rajputs and their contemporary Muslim rulers have invariably always ended in the victory of the latter. They have lost to Ghazni, Ghori, Khilji, Babur, the Marathas and bulldozed over by the British. Even the mightiest Rajputs of lore have been greatly exaggerated by their successors, as Prithviraj Chauhan was captured while bolting from Tarain, Rana Sanga lost to Babur at Kanua and Rana Pratap lost at Haldighati, but the bards simply replaced history with fanciful legends. As for the

Chittor episode depicted in the film, it was a case of an emperor expanding his empire and annexing another kingdom to his in his quest to rival Alexander (Sikander), and had nothing to do with a quest to capture any beautiful woman. It was at best a minor incident in the illustrious career of Alauddin Khilji. There is no historical evidence of any such disenfranchised queen of unparalleled beauty called Padmini/Padmavati during this period, and there is even no evidence for the infamous jauhar being committed in Chittor during Khilji's invasion. It was only the later additions of lickspittle bards and courtiers that attempted to glean glory from an incident that happened long ago. In the film it is shown that Rawal Rattan Singh was treacherously betrayed by his own courtier, then abandoned by the other Rajputs, saved by his crafty wife, and yet overpowered (again treacherously) by Khilji's camp. Anyone with a cent of sense, and some knowledge of history, need only look at Alauddin Khilji's track record to see that he wasn't just a bloodthirsty tyrant he was made out to be. Chittor never stood much chance against the might of the calculating, smart warrior who repelled the Mongols several times, overthrew Jalaluddin Khilji and managed to expand and secure an empire as vast as he did. He was a reliable ruler, competent at the least to manage such a huge enterprise as the Delhi Sultanate, and enacted many reforms that helped centralise power and consolidated what could have been a fractured and fractious kingdom full of rebellions. But alas, fact and reliable historical sources have never meant much to the Hindutva parrots who have trouble discerning myth from history, and based on the recent comments by Satyapal Singh about the lack of evidence for evolution because nobody has seen an ape turn into man, common sense is also a distant dream.

The greatest problem with Padmavat, apart from the islamophobia, pandering to the overblown Rajput pride and opportunism is the glorification of the act of Jauhar. As noted above, jauhar was the ceremonious act of self immolation on a funeral pyre by some north Indian Hindu cultures in the past by the women of defeated kingdoms to protect the "honour" of the men who couldn't protect them. In this day and age, particularly in the wake of the #MeToo movement and the repeated issues of the security of women (or lack thereof) in this country, it is irresponsible and insensitive to portray this practice of self-mutilation as such a glorious and praise-worthy sacrifice. These women in the narrative have no agency in their lives. Even the consistently brilliant Padmavati, who is shown as the embodiment of everything womanly, noble, pious, and virtuous, and frequently makes the smartest decisions, has no option but to jump into the sacrificial pyre, and people are supposed to celebrate the fact that in this world of the ideal Hindu culture women are nothing more than their wombs, and their lives are not worth more than the honour of the men in their lives. I could go on about the feminist issues, and the gender biases, the saffronisation of the culture and all at length, but the film hides none of it so it's easy to pick up on anyway.

Padmavat could have been that rare Bollywood movie epic that elevated Indian cinema to global standards of cinema, but opts to hide behind grandiose visuals, reductive storytelling, underdeveloped characters and uninspired musical accompaniment. Borrowing liberally from *Game of Thrones* and *Baahubali* can only get you so far, and an over-reliance on numbingly extravagant VFX, and the gratuitous sucking-up to the present political climate mars an otherwise enjoyable picture. Hopefully Bhansali has learnt his lesson (where the very community he tried to celebrate turned on him and made his magnum opus a nightmare) and will henceforth look for better material from better people who aren't as fickle as fame, and makes better pictures that do not assault the senses but wraps us up and carries us away to the story· that he can undoubtedly tell without reliance on Deeepika's tears, her makeup and costuming, and the chiselled abs and raw sexuality of his male leads. Sometimes, restraint can be the greatest asset, along with some sense and understanding.

The Queer Experience of a Small-Town Indian

2018

[This article was originally published by *The Covai Post* as part of their TCP's LGBTQ Pride effort.]

When did I realise I was queer? I never had an epiphany of any sort that revealed to me that's what I was. I always thought of myself as just another little boy, perhaps a little more gifted than others (as one does in the days of infinite self-worth before life slaps you in the face). I remember my mother telling me that I was always fascinated by the long hair on one of my cousin-sisters as a toddler, and how I used to sit behind her and drape her hair over mine and admire the oiled Malayali magnificence as it cascaded past my shoulders. And later, there was the mimicking of the Siva-tandava from the TV serial on the deity. Even as a young child, every single one of my idols were female, starting with the heroine of childhood mythology lessons from the family, the devi Durga. Then came the Hindi and Malayalam actresses who mesmerised me with their eyes on screen, be it Shobana in *Manichitrathazhu*, Divya Unni in *Aakashaganga*, or Raveena Tandon and Pooja Batra with their long legs and alluring dance moves. It was always the actresses I danced to, always the female identities I aligned myself with. And this inevitably led to towels pinned over my head in place of their long flowing locks, and bed sheets replacing the sarees and skirts, lehengas and cholis. There were so many times my mother walked in on me prancing around with ornately arranged towels on my head, and yelled at me to not do it. But she was never accusatory in her tone, or ever tried to shame me. Back then, I myself might have felt ashamed of it and hidden that part from all eyes for years, well into my teens, but looking back now, it was more her trying to protect me from the world rather than asking me to change for her or myself. Did she have an inkling back then? This was the 90s, and queerness was an alien concept for every-day Malayali adults, let alone children. I was just a child expressing himself, and everyone in the family was used to the femininity that was inherent in most of my choices, and I don't remember ever being shamed for it. May be some of them might have questioned me on it and told me to try something different, my brother might have told me to not always dance to girly songs, but none of that has remained in my memory because it never mattered to me, or left deep unhealable scars because their love and support of me as a person always outweighed everything else.. I was a child, and I was living my best self. The only regret was that I never could get a doll to play with, but then again, I never got around to getting that wooden model of a KSRTC bus to play with either. In school, I don't remember ever feeling ostracised or separate from the others, even when I viewed the world in what I see now as a slightly different shade than what I assume the other boys did. It was the little things. In those days, boys and girls didn't mix, but I was always friends with the girls, be it in 1st standard while playing house during the last period games, or in 4th-5th standard when I was placed in the midst of the girls in class as punishment for talking during school hours. That was punishment for the other boys, who recoiled from the girls like they had rabies, but I was completely at ease with them, because I didn't see the duelling natures of gender that we were being fed at home and in school, consciously or unconsciously. I was supposed to feel uncomfortable and shameful, but all I felt was that I could do whatever I did with the boys without the judgement I might get.

But of course, growing up teaches you things about the world and breaks the tinted glasses you viewed it through until then. In my teens, I was in a boarding school setting, and that heavily influenced how I perceived the world and myself. Again, there was a constant separation between the sexes, by the school authorities (who seemed to think that any two people of the opposite gender interacting would lead to orgies or something), and by the boys themselves who had the hard job of being infatuated with girls and at once being confused about them. But here, for the first time, I was made to feel bad about my feminine traits, and made to feel that I wasn't man enough. I was obviously feminine, and I got the usual teasing that nearly all queer people have experienced in some way, shape or form, from classmates and seniors, and even the faculty. I distinctly remember when I was 13, in English class (which was taught by my favourite teacher), I must have acted particularly feminine, because she looked at me and chided me, saying "What are you, a *Chandupottu*? (The slur was based on the Malayalam film of the same name, which portrayed an effeminate man and his journey to become a "real" man). That cut deep, especially coming from someone who I considered ideal and infallible. I felt soiled and dirty, almost tainted by the touch of femininity. From that day, I tried actively to act more masculine (I don't know how successful I was at this, but another teacher later did comment on how I no longer acted "like a girl"). No one could really fault me for anything else, because I was undoubtedly one of the better students in the school, having good grades and always winning prizes for both artistic and athletic activities. But I always felt inadequate, because I was viewing myself as at fault for being feminine. My teens in that atmosphere was further complicated with the question of sexuality, when by the age of 14 I came across the word Queer in the newspaper, and I realised that there was a name for what I felt. That was the first time I felt different because of who I felt attracted to.

Being a queer individual from a small-town in Idukki, Kerala could have been hell in many ways, but somehow I have managed to navigate it better than most would have. Maybe it's the fact that I never questioned my queerness. It was always apparent to me that I was queer, but while early on I tried to stifle my femininity and sexuality, I was aware of the outside world enough, I had read extensively enough to know that there was nothing inherently wrong with being queer, and whatever issue there could be would be based on the perceptions of the people and institutions around me. And I actively tried to shape those perceptions around me in order for me to navigate these social institutions I was thrust into. After a near mental breakdown around the age of 16, I had resolved to actively try and spread awareness around me at least so that life could be that little bit easier for me. In high school, I made sure that my friends were always aware that sexist and queer-bashing humour or discussions were not something they could partake in around me, and being a person with some amount of clout, I did manage that with my closest circles. I came out to many of my friends, and while many were shocked, none were truly appalled or horrified, and none of them ever pushed me away because of the revelation. That seems an impossibility to most young queer people from rural areas, because the ignorance around them can be crippling. That gave me validity, and a sense of hope that even though I was in such a small-town environment, awareness and education could help. I was still terrified of coming out to my family, because I worried that they would be disappointed, but I knew that even if they were, I had the choice to step out on my own as an individual, because my parents had always instilled in their children the value of independence and individuality, and I'm forever grateful for that. Of course, there were a few instances that didn't leave a great taste in my mouth, and they came from surprising places. There was that time one group of boys teased me about them not feeling safe with a 'predator' like me walking around while they were practising shirtless, and I did feel deeply hurt, but the fact that the guy who said that came up to me, owned up to his mistake and apologised on his own volition helped in our reconciliation. It clearly stemmed from a place of ignorance and chauvinism, and a conversation helped in clearing the misconceptions. The other time was when a counselling session was arranged for the students by the school, where we could voluntarily sign up to speak with the therapist. Well, I wasn't surprised when the nun who was the therapist shrivelled up and nearly fainted when I came out to her (after she had been praising me about my grades and everything), and I felt more tickled than incensed when she couldn't even form a coherent sentence after that.

Coming out as queer to my family didn't become the melodrama I envisioned it to be. My mother asked me, while I was in college, and I said that I was queer. That was that. There were no hysterics, no blame-games or tears. Of course, she being an Indian mother, worried about who will look after me when I'm old and lonely, and about "log kya kahenge", but there was never an accusation from her. She had the foresight to do research online before asking me, and I can't explain the pride I feel in that woman who sets such a great example for me. My parents have always been more informed and open than many of the parents of my peers, and we have established relationships as adults where we as children know we have the option to be open and honest with them. My mother is practical enough to know that our society has yet to catch-up, and might not be as accepting as her, so she would love to see me independent and settled abroad where I can be myself without fear of being targeted (she doesn't know that my personality might be a bigger issue). The bigger hurdle was my brother, who already knew what was up, but wasn't ready to accept it. We have always been as close as siblings can be, so I knew he was more worried about what could happen to me rather than seeing problems for himself and the family when he refused to accept my queerness. There was a period when the issue was bubbling under the surface, but once I made him understand that it wasn't a phase or a deliberate choice, he seems to be satisfied as long as I'm happy, and I can't be selfish and ask for more. As for the extended family, I literally couldn't care less about who thinks what, because it's not their business how I live my life. That has always been my approach to dealing with my queerness. Paraphrasing Rupaul, unless they pay my bills, I can't be bothered to pay any mind to what others think of me. That's beyond my control and I can't spend my life worrying about inconsequential things like that. Family will always come first if the relationships are strong, and I believe in at least some of them to know that and understand that.

For me, the journey to my present state of mind has been more about finding peace within myself than my struggles with the outside world. Body dysmorphia, low self-esteem, bouts of depression and other struggles are a constant companion, and of course the current rise of fundamentalism in all fields of Indian culture has me worried, but things that are beyond one's control cannot, and should not, govern one's life. Fact remains that the paradigms for small-town queer people are different from those in the big cities. The queer rural experience is fundamentally rooted in ignorance, of the individual themselves and the people around them. The idea of queerness is alien, and concepts like homosexuality, bisexuality, asexuality et al are completely beyond the comprehension of the people, because there is no visibility or awareness for anything queer-related in this world. There are no identifiable icons that young queer persons can identify with, and the education that they have about sex and sexuality is laughable at best. The social agencies that exercise most authority in the lives of people, be it education, politics, religion or entertainment and media, all of them are generally extremely negative towards any notions of queerness, and denunciations are quick and constant. There is close to no literature that is available at the disposal of questioning youngsters. What this leads to is an inevitable self-hatred or aversion that results in unhealthy suppression of sexuality. The constant barrage of derogatory or comical portrayal of queerness in the influential media of entertainment makes it far easier for young queer individuals to turn inward and hate themselves for being "bad" or "dirty". There is also the belief amongst a lot of queer people from rural areas that sex is all that queerness is about, and there is no concept of queer pride, community or universality. So most simply think about the next secret dalliance to satiate a hunger they don't fully understand, and cannot fathom that there is more than they envisioned. They do not know words like gay, bisexual, pansexual etc as sexual identities, but possibly only as slurs. Then there is a definite feeling of inferiority for those queer individuals who do have more awareness about sexuality and gender, when they see that the few spaces that do cater to people of their tribe are for people they can't equate with; the shiny and beautiful urban rich. The unattainable nature of a city nightlife, the uncompromising standards of physical beauty and material worth and a constant feeling of not being represented in any way (even in the few instances in mainstream media, we only get to see the lives of upper-middle class youth with perfect bodies and boutique-ready faces) makes even the most aware rural queer person feel separated by invisible lines. Being from a small town, the chances of sexual encounters are surprisingly ample in this age of smartphones and more, but as someone who has no interest in anonymous hook-ups or instant gratification, life can be a drag in many ways. There's not much of a queer culture, even though there are Facebook groups and such of queer individuals aimed at bolstering communication and a feeling of belonging, but the fact that queerness is still considered a taboo, and in fact very much illegal in our country means that being open is a dangerous game without allies in everyday life. While I have great queer friends, it's depressing when there really isn't much chance to hang out as human beings and experience the human comforts of regular conversations and such with people you identify with more easily. There's always an invisible wall that separates me from every other person in my life, and the few people who could walk through and engage are big-city boys in completely different paradigms. But these few friends that I do have, the bonds I have nurtured with these fellow queer individuals are incredibly strong and unique to this world of the queers, because we get to choose our own families in a way, and I have a brotherhood that I cherish very much, because I know they understand the struggles and unique experiences we share better than anyone else. If nothing else, it's always great to have a group of people to be unabashedly queer with, watch *Rupaul's Drag Race* with and sing along badly to Beyoncé and Celine Dion.

I might be an anomaly in terms of small-town queer boys, because I never went through a questioning or self-hating phase because of my sexuality. I have always looked outside, feeling always as an outsider, and my world has always been the greater world outside my semi-urban hometown in the wilds of Idukki. Books, TV, Internet- every single aspect of the modern age that brings the world closer to home has been used so that I haven't had to grapple with small-town mindsets about queerness and sexuality, and that has helped me as a person in becoming independent and individualistic in my own expression of queerness. I can question gender norms with my choices without feeling ostracised by others, because I have trained myself to see my queerness as part of myself and not as a construct in opposition to others and their vision. Where once, I was ashamed of my femininity, I now have accepted and started celebrating the glory of femininity in each person, and I try to teach that to my colleagues and friends, so that in turn they can go out into the world a little more aware and accepting. I have made it so that my sexuality isn't all I am, it's just part of who I am as a whole. Where once I had to watch how I walked and talked, and how I leaned forward so as not to appear too effeminate, now I paint my nails (because boys could and should be allowed to be fabulous), grow my hair long and keep a beard, and never shy away from the natural exaggerations of my gestures or facial expressions. Being masculine and feminine are not mutually exclusive, and neither is inferior or superior, and if people realise that simple fact, then that's already a great leap forward not just in terms of queerness and gender identity, but also for the erasure of the chauvinistic bases of Indian society. All that is just a part of who the whole person is, and not the person themself.

My colleagues, my friends and I have long discussions on topics of gender and sexuality, and while initially there might be a little hesitancy, I have found that with the right attitude, people do want to learn more and educate themselves, and it's the arrant ignorance that is really the root of all the homophobia that has taken hold in our society. The biggest struggle for small-town boys, in my experience at least, is the lack of awareness and discussions that could enlighten the people, queer and otherwise. The queer population only see their queerness as a sexual deviancy that they have to practise in hiding, behind veils and shadows because it is abhorrent and deviant, and that attitude births a population who are all about anonymous sex and unfettered and innate anti-feminine attitudes, because it is seen as undesirable and reprehensible. That needs to change.

As a 25 year old queer man from a little town in the foothills of Idukki, my experience might not be unique or original, but the personal flavours and individual choices that lead to where I am today surely differentiate it from typical urban or rural queer existence. It occupies a limbo stage, neither cosmopolitan, nor totally ignorant and backward and oppressive. But every story has value, and these stories need to be heard, I guess, so that other small-town boys can identify with them and see themselves as being able to see a valid and legitimate future that's not limited to what they could envision in their small-town worlds, and that can only be a good thing.

Hindutva and Hinduism : The Rise of Fundamentalism In Modern India

2018

Today, in India, proclaiming you are a Hindu is considered tantamount to declaring your public allegiance to the Sangh Parivar, and the Hindutva movement propagated by the ruling BJP government and its affiliates. This new reactionary strain of Hinduism, popularly called Hindutva, has drastically altered perceptions of what it means to be Hindu. To consider this cosmetically revamped Hindutva notion of Hinduism with the historical Hindu cultures and religion (for lack of a better word) is egregious, erroneous and highly detrimental to the status of Hinduism as an inclusive and constantly evolving entity, as well as negating its long and rich history. How did this happen, that a Hindu is now required to be defined and categorised by rigid guidelines and criteria, and they have to abide by some (questionable) set of practices and ideals to be considered a "real Hindu"? When did Hinduism, considered one of the more ancient religions still in wide practice, become just a pale imitation of Judaic religions, with the tendencies for inflexibility and fundamentalist practices and rigid internal structures that govern what is and what isn't, what should and what shouldn't entail Hinduism? What exactly is Hindutva, and how does it affect, relate to and differ from Hinduism in its original sense? Through personal inquiries and experience, I will try to grapple with and answer these questions and others to the best of my ability so that I can reconcile the practical, scientific mindset of a 21st century Indian with the rich cultural heritage that has been given to me as the legacy of the Hindu culture I was raised in.

Defining Hinduism is a fool's errand, because the very essence of Hinduism defies definitions. While a Western understanding of it is as a religion, Hinduism is not just a religion, as it is also a set of varied cultures, practices, beliefs and ideas that do not have an ecclesiastical order, an hierarchy of formal authority, official governing body, definite set of prescribed laws to be followed, a unanimously approved head or prophet whose words are considered incontestable or any holy book that acts as the voice of God or the central scripture. A Hindu has the freedom to worship any which way he likes, being polytheistic, pantheistic, monotheistic, agnostic or atheistic in his beliefs, and they do not have to worship at specific times or in specific places of worship alone. What we call Hinduism is an amalgamation of various different cultures and practices of different peoples that have been tentatively viewed together based on geographical and historical reasons quite separate from the actual practice of the 'religion' itself, because Hinduism is the culture, history and way of life of many different societies that have occupied the Indian subcontinent in the past two millennia or so. The historically Western understanding of India and Hindu cultures is severely lacking in grasping what they're dealing with and the extrapolation of

Abrahamic religious ideals and strictures over something far older and occupying a different paradigm has led to considerable confusion and misunderstanding of Hinduism internationally. In the modern sense of the word, Hinduism as a religion (as seen in popular media and public imagination) is the Vedic iteration tempered by the Bhakti tradition that influenced it a thousand year after Christ's purported birth. It also happens to be mainly focused on the North Indian version of the religion, particularly of the heartland of Uttar Pradesh and its adjoining states, while other regional and equally valid iterations of Hinduism hardly get any recognition in the outside world (more on the social and political implications of that later).

The generally accepted birth of Hinduism in its recognizable form is the Vedic age between 1900 BC and 1400 BC, the period after it being the age in which Hinduism as it is seen in its popular form takes shape along with its sister religions Buddhism and Jainism (both these religions also have been reabsorbed back into the *pallu* of Mother Hinduism, who is always benevolent and all-accepting at least until the modern day). It is said to have reached a "Golden Age" during the Gupta Empire (the Puranic age of Hinduism), which also gave rise to the monotheistic traditions of the Bhakti Movement like Shaivism and Vaishnavism between 200 BC and 500 CE. The Bhakti movement prospered and grew during the later times of Hindu and Islamic rulers, and the reform movements during the British occupation forced Hinduism into the modern times and asked it to forego many of its questionable practices like sati. Hinduism as a religion and culture was constantly in a state of evolution, reflecting the social and political changes happening within the Indian subcontinent throughout its history, and by adapting to circumstances and adopting new practices, by moulding itself to suit the needs of the people, society and the times, Hinduism has been able to successfully navigate multiple catastrophic changes in political fortunes in the subcontinent without significant decrease in its adherence or practice, which itself is quite a unique thing for all the religions in existence today. The fact that practices and symbols in the Hindu religion today can be traced back to the days of the Indus Valley civilization some 3200 years ago shows that it has mostly been a constantly updated set of different indigenous cultural practices and ways of life that just happened to be amalgamated in time under this umbrella term. Vedic Hinduism also has distinct similarities with Zoroastrianism, owing to their origins from the Proto-Indo-Iranian cultures. For the simplest and most obvious example, both religions have the concepts of positive and negative entities constantly in opposition to each other; for Hindus they are the good Devas and the evil Asuras, and the Zoroastrians have the inverse form with the good Ahura and evil Daevas. It would do well for any Hindu today to read up on the long history and origins of Vedic Hinduism, and how its journey from that time to the present day has shaped what we practise today instead of blindly accepting what we hear from our possibly ill-informed and biassed elders.

Hindutva can be summarised as a reactionary radicalised version of the Vedic religion that finds its identity in opposition to the two other major religions of the world, Islam and Christianity. It aims at making Hinduism into a solid entity with a definite set of rules of practice and a systematic approach to worship and which wants to define who can be and who can't be a Hindu. Anyone who knows anything about Hinduism can spot the obvious flaws in this notion from miles away, but apparently dogmatism, ignorance, fiery rhetoric and a healthy hatred for Islam and Christianity can be powerful tools to manipulate the masses into believing any arrant nonsense, based on the situation in the country presently. What the BJP and Sangh Parivar have done is systematically alter people's perceptions of what it means to be Hindu, what it takes to be a Hindu and who can be a Hindu, and this also means that all those who they deem to be NOT Hindus are not Indian and thus have no place in deciding the future of the country and the people in it. Mixing politics, history and culture in such a muddle has left people confused and confounded, unable to form logical statements to define and oppose the statements of the Bhakts without in some way contradicting some other valid point of their own. This is probably their cleverest trick, and we must get ourselves educated and aware enough to see through these smoke-screens and use logic and common sense, and a little bit of historical awareness, to successfully navigate the swamps they have the people trapped in. Before defining who is a Hindu or an Indian, we must be able to adequately understand who we are as a Hindu or an Indian, and what makes us Indian or a Hindu based on lived experiences.

One of the main strengths of Hinduism as a religion is that it wasn't ever an insecure religion. Unlike, say Christianity, Hinduism never lays claim to being The One Righteous Path to salvation, or hails itself as the only way to God (and we can get into the Hindu concept of God in the following section). The basic tenets of Hinduism or the Hindu Dharma makes it clear that it considers itself more of a source for inspiration rather than a strict guideline to be followed to obtain a place in a better dimension. Thus being rid of the narrow view of being the sole path to heaven, Hinduism never had any trouble accepting the validity of other religions as alternate paths to a common goal. The existence and spread of all the major religions in the world within the Indian subcontinent is blatant testament to the accepting nature of Hinduism, which in turn considers any religion to be an extension of itself in many ways, like a different path, perhaps a little long-winded and turbulent, but still leading towards the same destination. Obviously, as history testifies, the fundamental ideas of Christianity and Islam cannot tolerate contradiction or competition to their self-proclaimed status as the One True Faith and this has led to so many conflicts that have shaped human history. Even today, the Christian fervour of conversions is a major concern to the Hindutva brigade, who use it as an example of the inability of the Hindu to stand up for himself in the same way as a Christian, because there is no concept of conversion in Hinduism that would sever a person from the absent fundamental structures of Hinduism. Christianity and Islam both are militant religions in many ways, eager to amass more and more people to its fold by hook or crook. I remember the incident my mother told me when I was younger, of how the poor women in Kotdwara (a small town in Uttarakhand) were required to convert to Christianity if they were to get employment in the church or its affiliated institutions (including the school). While it isn't forcing someone blatantly, twisting their hands for financial reasons is far from the honest teachings that these missions are supposed to be celebrating. The promise of food and employment always wins over any other allegiance in the end. In Kerala, particularly in my district of Idukki, there's a running joke that if there's a high place in sight, there would be a cross upon it (because of the overzealous nature of the churches to always have the most visible, higher ground reserved for them with said crosses, be it in the uninhabited wilds of the forest or in the middle of a city). Where the Hindutva brigade succeeds is in converting deep resentments against the Christians and Muslims that has been growing within the heart of Hindus over the blatantly biased nature the three peoples are treated in politics etc.

In Hinduism, man isn't the centre of the universe. That would be tantamount to blasphemy to the Christian concept of the universe, where the anthropomorphized God (usually represented as a wizened old man with a full beard, typically Caucasian) created Man in his own image, then fashioned women out of a rib and created everything else to be subordinate to them. In Hinduism, man is just part of the universe, and his life force or *jeevaatma* is part of the *paramatma*, as with every other life form on Earth. Everything is thus equalised, sentient or not, plant or animal. This means that a Hindu can envision 'God' in anything, because everything is encompassed by that godliness. When a Hindu speaks of the 33 million gods of his religion, laymen might believe it to be individual gods but the actuality is that these are just personal representations of 'God' as envisioned by each individual. This always confounds Western discourse, because a Hindu has the freedom to identify his personal deity in anything he wishes to, in any form he wishes to and any time he wants to, whereas a Christian always has to worship the white-man's God, and to a lesser extent the image of a white-washed Jesus Christ. While most westerners only see the elephant-headed Ganapathy or the ape Hanuman when he thinks of Hindu gods, and might at best equate it to remnants of a pagan animal-worshipping past, what it actually speaks to is the rich tradition of inclusivity and pluralism within the many religions and practices that have fused together over the aeons to become what Hinduism is today. A Hindu isn't required to follow the strict sayings of any 'Holy Book' to be able to worship his personal deity to any level of devotion they might yearn to. One could be in temples every day, know the Gita by-heart and recite hymns like taking a breath and yet he is no more a Hindu than a man who never takes one step in the temple his entire life and yet has the name of Krishna on his lips when he wakes up or goes to sleep.

Each person has the licence to worship an *ishta devta*, and these often reflect the personalities of the persons involved, because one always appeals to that idea which seems closest to the likelihood of granting one's wishes. For example, my mother is devoted to Lord Krishna, especially his infant form as housed in the Sree Krishna Swamy temple in our hometown of Thodupuzha, while my brother is an ardent follower of Lord Siva, the volatile destroyer of worlds. I myself used to be all for the devi Durga, one of the martial representations of the feminine energy (Shakthi), until later in life when I transferred that same devotion to living women who exemplify the ideals that appear divine to me and who attain levels of super-human with their talent, humanity and work-ethic. An extended version of this can also be seen in the tradition of family temples, where one family or a group of families are devoted to the deity of a particular temple in the area and consider the divinity there as a guardian of said family.

The Hindutva ideal of Hinduism is very much a north Indian vision of the religion, where the God-king Ram attains supreme status along with Lord Krishna, and if one pays close attention to their rhetoric, it is all based on this narrow regional iteration of a religion far too diverse and dynamic to be thus represented. They would have the Gita as the holiest of holy texts, supposed to be taken as literally as Christians and Muslims take the Bible and Quran respectively, without an ounce of irony. They would have it turned into a homogenous mess that would enable the few to lead the many, in the same way of the Abrahamic religions. That's just stupid, and I have no problems calling it out as such.

The success of Hinduism, which enabled it to survive multiple foreign invasions and even the vampiric British occupation, has been its ability to evolve, adapt, adopt and change. One of the central ideas in Hindu philosophy is the fact of perennial change, of the constant flux of fortunes and the concept of cyclic birth and death. This means that traditionally, and there is ample historical evidence for this, Hinduism has always been able to modify itself to represent and help the people of the times rather than simply asking them to blindly follow outdated ideals and beliefs. The Hindu religion and culture has been in a state of constant evolution and updation, taking whatever enriches it from within and eschewing outdated, unnecessary and dangerous practices in favour of those which benefit and speak to the people.

From the Vedic age itself, this characteristic is evident. As mentioned earlier, the Proto-Indo-Iranian cultural influence on Hinduism is obvious, and later when it became too rigid in its structure, it gave birth to Buddhism and Jainism, which in turn enriched its progenitor with many new and outstanding ideas. The Bhakti movement, the Puranic tradition, the concept of *Dasavatara* (the ten incarnations of Lord Vishnu), the Turkic and Islamic influences because of the many Muslim monarchies, the reformists of the 20th century; all of these varied factors have helped in keeping Hinduism as an actively growing and changing religion. The pantheon of Hindu gods themselves are a representation of this evolution. From the Vedic age to the Puranas, the Itihasas (epics like *Mahabharatha* and *Ramayan*a) and in the later writings, we see how new gods are added, regional deities are co opted and outsider cultures are embraced; at first we have the devas like the lightning lord Indra, the fire god Agni, the wind god Vayu etc, who represent the elemental forces of nature with Shakthi being symbolic of the feminine which is the originator of life itself. The tribal chieftain (and possibly Indus Valley originated) Rudra was merged with Siva and added to the pantheon at a later date just like the suddenly all-powerful Vishnu to make the trio of Brahma-Vishnu-Maheshwara. Has nobody wondered why those three are considered the greatest of Hindu gods, and yet Indra is the Lord of all Gods? The answer is fairly simple; Indra and his ilk were earlier gods who were supplanted by the later gods in popularity (just think of Raj Kapoor being completely overshadowed in today's social consciousness before fan-favourites like Shahrukh, Amir and Salman Khan). Later came the likes of Rama and Krishna, who could possibly have been real individuals deified much later and elevated to godliness. Just imagine, if it can happen to Jayalalitha and Rajnikanth in Tamil Nadu in the last 50 years, it's not hard to fathom the devotion of much more primitive and unenlightened commoners of the centuries ago. Hell, the recent *Padmavati* movie controversy exposed something similar, where the fictional character of Rani Padmini from Malik Jaisi's metaphorical poem came to be worshipped both as a goddess, as well as believed to be the forbearer of certain ill-informed Rajput peoples. Regional traditions were constantly added to the classical Hindu religion as well, best exemplified by the differences of Hinduism as practised in North India and South India. In Kerala and Tamil Nadu, for a quick example, Lord Shiva and Lord Vishnu united to have the child Ayyappan, who later became the adopted son of the Raja of Pandalam and presently is probably the biggest addition to the Hindu pantheon along with Murugan (another son of Siva, this time legitimate) from the south. The differences in the practices of worship, celebrations and mythologies of the North and South are far too numerous to enumerate here, the simplest being the existence of the groves (or *kavu*) devoted to the serpentine spirits of nature and ancestors that all Hindu temples have in Kerala (and even without temple association in many cases) which you won't find anywhere north of the Deccans.

The Hindutva agenda, though, clearly doesn't know its own history, or chooses to ignore it. It aims for uniformity and homogeneity in the same vein as Christianity so that it is easier to separate what is and what isn't Hindu. But Hinduism isn't just a religion, it is also inseparably tied into the fabric of the national identity and cultural history of the people who reside in the subcontinent. The Hindutva tendencies to take everything literally and at face value have cheapened Hinduism into a joke. We have so many politicians spouting nonsensical "facts", like using the myth of the Kaurava births as factual evidence of test-tube babies in the Vedic age and the mention of the *Pushpaka Vimana* as evidence of the ability of flight in Indian antiquity that actual achievements by the ancient Indians are also being treated with equal disdain. They hanker for a golden age, a Rama Rajya, of purported perfection and superiority and take heavily philosophical texts like the Gita and the Upanishads (and extremely outdated ones like the misogynistic Manusmriti) very literally without grasping even the minutest of metaphors. They say they want to return India to its golden age before the coming of foreign invaders and contaminators like the Sultanates and the Mughals, but forget the fact that such a utopian India never existed, and India has always been a set of varied peoples and cultures occupying this subcontinent through tenuous connections at best coming under the umbrella term of Hinduism (which really means the ways of the people of the Sindhu if people think about for a second) that have been constantly changing and evolving as time goes by and new things are added to it. The Hindutva tendency is to do its own Brahminization of history, of reshaping and "correcting" historical facts in ways that benefit their extremely narrow notions of Hinduism. An obvious example would be celebration of the Marathas and Rajputs while the Mughals are depicted as deplorable alien invaders, when the historical evidence clearly paints the Mughals as a truly Indian empire at least from the days of Akbar the Great, who always celebrated the local traditions and accepted the ways of the people as their own, had many Hindus in his court and even married Rajput women. Their many contributions to enriching the culture, literature, art, music etc. of the subcontinent is quietly pushed under the rug while inaccurate portrayals of them as evil leeches who terrorised their subjects and the Hindu kings of the time have gained vogue, and much celebration among the ruling faction (using school textbooks to this use to devastating effect, and social media is another tool they effortlessly deploy). Take the example, once again, of the depiction of Alauddin Khilji, the sultan of Delhi and the biggest political and military figure of his age as a savage charlatan barely better than a beast in the historically blasphemous *Padmavati*, while the ineffectual and bickering petty kings of Rajputana are celebrated as honourable and deified when in reality the annexation of Chittor was nothing more than a minor campaign at best for the man who pushed back the Mongols several times.

What the Hindutva brand of Hinduism does is turn people into ignorant and misinformed hordes of mindless minions capable of attacking innocent children in school buses in the name of a film, or murderers capable of lynching Muslims or dalits in the name of correcting nonexistent "wrongs", like trafficking cows or marrying outside their caste. It is turning an open and accepting religion and its people into a fundamentalist, radical population incapable of informed inquiry or discussions, and injecting male chauvinism, homophobia, casteism, sectism, xenophobia and regionalism into their minds in the name of religious fervour while actually only benefitting the political machinations of a Machiavellian regime.

The rise of Hindutva can be said to be in reaction, as I mentioned earlier, to the bias felt by the ordinary Hindu population in small towns and cities in particular towards Christians and Muslims. It is the same kind of usually repressed resentment towards others that enabled a buffoon like Donald Trump to win the presidency of the US, because he voiced the unpopular opinions unapologetically. Just a cursory conversation with my family, all of whom are ardent BJP supporters I'm sad to say, has given me some of the perceived injustices that they believe are turning Hindus towards the BJP and the Parivar because they believe that only they care about Hindus and their needs. There's the subsidisation of Hajj for Islamic pilgrims, while the infrastructure at Hindu places of worship like Haridwar, Sabarimala etc. are often neglected entirely. Sabarimala is an immediately identifiable issue because it is the biggest place of pilgrimage in Kerala, around 15 million devotees flocking to the hilltop shrine every year during the *Makaravilakku* celebrations in particular, but still the roads are ill-maintained, the infrastructure is at best serviceable and the services and facilities provided to the devotees are subpar. And yet, all the income from said temple is pumped into the government treasury overseen by the ministry while very little of it ever comes back to the benefit of the temples themselves or to the community, while the churches and mosques aren't required to do the same. It has been a recent trend in even some small towns where Muslim patrons would only call upon Muslim autorickshaws, or visit shops owned only by Muslims, and turn Muslim neighbourhoods into completely alien territories where outsiders are made unwelcome. There are several examples of this in Malappuram especially which has earned it the unflattering name of Little Pakistan, where even Hindu and Christian patrons cannot avail restaurants or refreshments during the Ramzan season. Traditionally, a Hindu society had never been reclusive or exclusive based on religious lines, as evidenced by the happy coexistence of all communities in nearly all the towns and villages in my home state of Kerala, where temples rub shoulders with churches and mosques and all devotees gather for the celebrations and festivals of any religion quite happily and freely, but in recent times, the Othering of dissimilar peoples by all religions has led to very strained relations which are often reflected even in the small things. Years of such built up resentment among the Hindu population, who have felt uninvested in by the politicians and the powerful in favour of the far more structurally organised religions has now started to take shape in the form of support to the twisted fantasies vomited by the Sangh Parivar. Their version of history is misinformed, their "scientific" discoveries of the ancients are a joke at best, insults to intelligence at worst, their vision of the future misguided and their means crooked and inflammatory. We have become intolerant people, who can't let a cinematic depiction of a fictional literary character be just that, a means of entertainment but have to torch buses and raise hell. Free speech has become tools of incendiary proclamations by the Parivar, and something denied to everyone else and artistic licence and appreciation has been brought down to bow at the feet of ignorant and belligerent crowds of thugs. It reminds one of the early stages of the Taliban or the Islamic State, which transformed the Islamic religion into its notoriously backwards, chauvinistic and terribly restricting state today. It is a truly saddening truth that Hindutva has poisoned Hinduism from the inside. The all-embracing, constantly updating and ever-evolving religion that stood the test of time for thousands of years without significant losses to its numbers or principles has now become just another dogmatic, fundamentalist religion used by politicians to mobilise people and turn one person against another based on the most arbitrary reasons.

In this climate, how does a Hindu, one who doesn't swallow the bile forced down their throats by the Hindutva brigade, reconcile with his spirituality without feeling ashamed or angry at the state of India? While Hindu and India are terms that can be interchanged, because both basically mean the people of the Sindhu, the culture of the subcontinent and not the religion itself should be our focus. Religion and spirituality should be entirely personal affairs. It should be the distinctly personal union between a person and the divine (whichever form of divinity they chose to worship or not), and people should be able to understand and interpret the teachings of each religion based on their intellect and life experiences and apply them to make not just their own lives, but those of the ones around them a little better. Hinduism doesn't have insecure gods who demand people to praise them and love them and pay tribute to them like an

American teenager, but the divinity within everything that can be appreciated and acknowledged. A Hindu does not mean just the followers of the *sanatana dharma*, or the religion itself, but all the many and varied peoples who occupy what is now the political boundary of modern India, because Hindu is the culture and civilization of this land, and no person here can separate themselves from it and pay allegiance to something that they have no direct inheritance to. The Hindu religion might be practised by the population, just like Christianity or Islam, but people of all faiths must remember that they are first and foremost part of this long and rich Hindu cultural heritage, one that has been unbroken since the Vedic age, enriched by the later additions by other foreign and internal differences. The responsibility isn't solely on the practitioners of the Hindu religion alone to accept the traditions of the Hindu culture. Christians and Muslims in India must also realise that their religions are only part of who they are, not the entirety of what they are.

Keralite Christians and Muslims have a much older tradition of both religions than the rest of the country and the idiosyncratic practices of these versions have been unique mixtures of the different religions and their encounter with the Hindu culture of this country, and that should be the example to be followed; not to simply ape the ways of the west in practices removed from the realities of the completely different paradigms we have in this country by evolving uniquely Indian (or Hindu) expressions of Christianity and Islam as the *Nasranis* and *Mappilas* of Kerala have done (until their reintroduction to the Western versions of the religions have brought new orthodoxy and fundamentalism to their numbers in recent times). They have to realise that their allegiance and kinship should be first and foremost to the people they share this land with, and their history with and not distant figures who have very little to do with their realities like the Pope in Rome or the practices of Sharia laws in culturally backward countries. All religions must move with the times and let their people grow and flourish as well. It's absolutely necessary that people of all faiths accept that they are first and foremost people of the Hindu cultural tradition (regardless of religious affiliation) and that India functions best as the multicultural, diverse and open nation it decided to be when it cut ties with Pakistan which elected to be a dogmatic and closed society instead. India needs to be secular, and secular doesn't mean that only a Hindu religious practitioner has to keep his religion as open and welcoming, but that all people have equal right to follow whichever form of the divine they wish to follow, and also the freedom not to follow any faith at all. That also must include Christians and Muslims who cannot close themselves out and consider themselves only as part of that Western tradition because that's a lie. The day people realise this, India can move forward, Hinduism can mend itself and the Hindu culture can reabsorb its wayward sisters into the fold once again and race into the modern age of secularism and openness.

P.S: Apparently Dr. Sashi Tharoor had some similar thoughts, and has written a brilliantly insightful book on the subject, which I have since read after the original publication of this article. I suggest everyone give the book a chance, because it is quite simply brilliant.

A Life in Pilgrimages

2020-2024

Growing up in India, particularly for those of us away from the major urban centres like Delhi or Mumbai, pilgrimages were a familiar part of our childhoods. I would even go so far as to say for most of us, these annual trips to distant religious institutions amounted to the only interesting vacation activity besides visiting cousins or grandparents. This was something to look forward to and often planned and anticipated well in advance. For the parents they may have been entirely about the spiritual and religious experience at least for me and I presume for most other kids it was more an opportunity to travel beyond the usual haunts, the chance to eat out at restaurants, to see unfamiliar sites and the possibility of souvenirs. It would also be a great story to tell your classmates after the holidays; something interesting to share and brag about and a new topic of conversation beyond the lives of cousins and relatives nobody cares about. In my little world of south-central Kerala we were mostly a collection of Christians and Hindus with more than enough fascinatingly alien destinations between the lot of us to be visited and discussed at length. I could be sharing stories about the jungles of Sabarimala while my friend talked to me about his trips to the calvary Mount or Malayattoor and we could both end up feeling the energy of exotic places we could not partake in ourselves.

My family was one of deeply devout Hindus. That meant that visits to temples, or *ambalam* as we call them, in our neighbourhood were almost a weekly if not a weekly activity when I was growing up. The one closest to my house was a temple dedicated to one of the Trimurtis, Lord Shiva that also housed Rudra and Vishnu as accompanying deities. When I was very young, there was a pooja and a *pratishtha* because the Shiva in the temple was lonely , and the priests had divined that in order to appease the lord his consort Parvathy must also be consecrated along with him. These gods thus had personalities, and each temple had a different interpretation or manifestation of the gods in the pantheon, themselves very much vibrant characters evolving over millennia. There were four other temples within five minutes driving distance from my house that we used to visit on special Hindu days, almost like mini pilgrimages. The first stop was always of course the Shiva temple in my village, then on to the Shiva temple of a more moody version near where my grandmother used to live. After that would be the Sree Krishna Swami temple in the middle of the town, where he was manifested as a younger version who was particularly beloved of mothers including mine and then finally on to the temple dedicated to the Goddess at the other end of town. This circuit was undertaken for most auspicious days or celebrations, be they birthdays, Vishu, Sivarathri, Deepavali or the individual festivals or *utsavam* of each temple.

The first real pilgrimage that involved travelling beyond the confines of my hometown that I distinctly remember was undertaken when I was still nearly a toddler. When we are around four years old, Malayali Hindu children go through the *Vidyarambham* or *Ezhuthiniruthu* ceremony that symbolically commences their introduction to the world of letters by propitiating the goddess Saraswati and the god Ganapathy. My parents took me to the Mookambika devi temple in the neighbouring state of Karnataka, a destination favoured by Malayalis. The temple is dedicated to all three goddess consorts, Saraswati, Parvathy and Lakshmi and is therefore considered especially auspicious for this ceremony. While I don't remember all the details of that trip, as we state a few days with one of my father's brothers in Mangalore for a few days and went to beaches and such that are also clashing for space in the vaul;ts of my ageing brain, I do remember sitting in the back of some car nas we drove down a dusty mountainside road overlooking a deep ravine with a river at the bottom. I also remember monkeys. I remember how there were a whole crowd of little boys like me sitting on the mandapam, the raised stone platform with carved pillars decorated with garlands of beautiful flowers. I was sitting in the lap of the older uncle, both of us clad in pristine white mundu, with a tray of sand in front of us. I remember the annoying little bald boy who was sitting next to me who couldn't stop fidgeting or complaining that got on my nerves pretty quickly. I remember my uncle clasping my little right fist in his and tracing the words "*Harishree ganapathaye namaha! Avighnamasthu!*" in the rice with my index finger three times. These are some of the oldest images etched in my memory, very vividly and with extraordinary detail.

The Sree Krishnaswamy temple in Guruvayur is a familiar name in every Malayali Hindu household, and so it was in mine. I can't honestly remember when the first time was when I went to this legendary place, but I dio believe it was during the period of time when we lived in Ernakulam for a few years. We took the train for this short journey, which was always an exciting prospect to me because it was a fancy and unusual way of travelling that surprisingly a lot of my friends hadn't experienced until well into their adulthoods or never at all. Guruvayur felt to me like such an intimidating place, with its large temple complex and the size of the area where we were queuing for entry, but my primary takeaway at that age were the shiny stalls along both sides of the queueing area that sold all kinds of chachkis. There were stalls selling incense, cheap imitation jewellery, ingredients for various poojas, pictures and idols of varying sizes of the Hindu pantheon but especially Krishna, accoutrements in brass and copper like bells, lamps and trays in traditional malayali style but the most important stalls were the ones that sold toys. They old toys you could buy at any ordinary temple utsavam from the makeshift seasonal stalls, including cheap plastic flutes and trumpets, balloons, cars, trucks, kitchen accessories etc but there were also fancier ones that I myself at least never could find in my hometown, including vehicles made out of metal or more details and durable plastic that always attracted me. Even though these upmarket toys were beyond our budget, the opportunity to wish, to envision a reality where I could own them, to touch them and then regretfully let go of them but still be satisfied with the experience of feeling them while I picked up something more reasonable was very special and part of the whole experience. The only ones that I remember still are little rubber balls, dense and aromatic in citrus shades that could bounce like the sentient blubber in their namesake movie. My brother and I both got one, and we did have a ton of fun with them in the days immediately afterwards.

We returned to Guruvayur for pilgrimage many times over the years, sometimes staying the night, including once for the wedding of one of my older cousins. That was a special treat. It was a rare opportunity for most of my father's side of the family to gather in one place and have a celebration together, all seven hundred thousand of us it seemed to my little mind. We had taken two luxury coaches and driven to Guruvayur, gossipping, sharing snacks, watching comedies and being ridiculous in ways we usually weren't in our everyday lives. The wedding ceremony itself was a little chaotic as the venue was extremely popular and busy, and there were several ceremonies going on at the same time like a relay race. The food provided there catered by someone associated with the temple I am presuming, was of course vegetarian but unusually ghastly (that may have something to do with the Thrissur style of the dishes) but on the way back in our couches, later at night, we stopped at a restaurant and gorged ourselves on porotta and egg roast. In those days, porotta in particular was a special indulgence only allowed on exceptional circumstances like this and therefore it stuck in my memory.

The last time I paid a visit to Guruvayur was most unusual. While all previous pilgrimages had been family obligations, this one was initiated by myself, much to the surprise of my mother. I hadn't been to the temple in nearly a decade, when one fine day I expressed a desire to go on this pilgrimage during my second year of college. I had recovered from a near fatal bout of Hepatitis only a few months prior, so my mother most likely imagined I had been overcome by a particularly strong wave of spiritualism. I had told her that I was only accompanying a friend who was desperate for me to join him, and that was partially true. I was indeed accompanying a friend, except that I had never met him in person before and had only known him virtually for a few weeks. We had found each other on a dating site which I had joined, and we had hit it off really well so when he asked if I could join him, I concurred without objection. As risk averse as I normally was, the dance with death had made me realise that I had to take more chances in life, and that the sad sorry state of my love life since I had been a teenager needed to be addressed. My final visit to Guruvayur thus far ended up being part travel, part pilgrimage and part first date.

There were three other locations that were frequented by my family during that period in my life when religious pilgrimages were part of it.

These were different from the more exotic and rare visits accomplished as life-goals, places that became significant because of how often we went or the specific reasons we undertook pilgrimages there. The most famous and oft-visited of them was the hill-top shrine of Sabarimala. Situated only a hundred kilometres from my hometown, this secluded shrine is dedicated to the lord *Ayyappan*, or *Manikantan* who is specifically favoured by the Dravidian language speaking people of southern India. This god is almost entirely absent from the northern pantheon of Hinduism. According to the legend associated with the temple, *Ayyappan* (also called *Dharmashasta*) was born from the union of two of the primary deities of the Hindu pantheon, Shiva and Vishnu in his female seductress form of Mohini. The child was then adopted by the royal family of Pandalam. The prince was asked to go in search of tiger's milk for his stepmother who pretended to be sick in order to exclude him from the line of succession thusly. After a number of adventures, the prince returned successful on tiger-back, and then retired to this spot to spend his remaining years as a celibate monk. The myths and legends are an amalgamation of puranic, local, tribal and shramanic ideas cobbled together over centuries with a brahmanical sheen plastered on top with later additions of folkloric and historical characters from the area. The asceticism of the deity recalls the traditions from Buddhism and Jainism that were extant in south India before the arrival of the brahmanic tradition, and could have been implanted on existing tribal deities as some of the forms of worship associated with this temple are quite unique and non-brahmanical.

To visit the shrine one has to be male, or a female outside the threshold of menstruation (pre-pubescent or after menopause). Devotees have to undertake a forty-one day fast, abstain from meat and alcohol, remain unshorn, wear a sacred necklace made of rudraksha or cheaper substitute beads and refrain from unclean thoughts, actions and words. During this period devotees are also required to wear traditional clothes in black, which means mundu and shirt for the men. The first of my pilgrimages to this fabled temple that attracts around 12 million visitors during the pilgrimage season of *Makara Vilakku* was undertaken around when I was ten. For this first milestone trip, my father, brother and I were joined by a pair of families from my neighbourhood with kids as well who were first-time "*Swamis*" like my brother and I. Being deemed a swami and following the prescriptions during the fasting period made me feel extra special, because it separated you from everyone else, especially at school. On the day of the trip, we went to the local temple and performed the lengthy rituals that were required before setting off, including consecration of the items needed for the bundles we were going to carry on our heads, containing such things as coconuts filled with ghee, puffed rice, flattened rice, jaggery etc called the *Thirumudikkettu*.

In my grandparents' day people used to walk hundreds of kilometres to get to the shrine, as do some deeply devout people still, but we took hired wheels to the Pamba river valley from where the trek up the mountain commences. There, we took a dip in this holy river as required before commencing the arduous trek. I remember distinctly how I found the water cool without being cold, but also very nearly filthy because of all the refuse from inconsiderate devotees over the years. The whole area had an air of unkempt chaos, with the ramshackle shops, devotees speaking many different languages hurrying along to or from the lord, stray dogs, donkeys and cattle rustling through the garbage etc. After taking the customary dip our party moved along with the throng of swamis going up to the summit, paying tribute to the various smaller shrines as we climbed up the mountainside, each of them important in its own way. The whole experience was fun for me, as I do think it was for the other children as well, as it was so unfamiliar from anything we had experienced so far in our short lives. The surroundings were alien, but even I could feel the sense of camaraderie and unity among the hundreds that climbed the sometimes twisting, sometimes paved, sometimes rutted mountain path in the shadows of tall tropical trees towards this young god we were all yearning to see. Every step of the trek, we chanted the name of the lord with our cries of "*Swamiye Sharanam Ayyappo*" and its many variants, and some small ditties as well which weer echoed by the others around us even if they weren't in our party. Unlike Guruvayur, there were no shops selling toys or souvenirs in this journey towards the lord. There were pit stops along the way selling water, fruits and access to restrooms for those in need. The adults in our party expected us kids to be tired and cranky after an hour or two of climbing but we were too excited by everything that was going on to give it a thought. I myself was too enthralled to notice. The views occasionally glimpsed over the edge were lovely, the constant chanting was calming and the company was fun.

We reached the summit around dusk, when the queuing started in earnest under the pavilions for the devotees leading to the temple complex. Once inside the compound, we unpacked the package on our heads to take out the necessities for the immediate rituals, and proceeded to the 18 steps wrought in solid gold that every swami needed to climb to reach his lord. The air was thick with the voices of hundreds as the line slowly made its way towards the central shrine, the *tirunada* also covered in gold, where Ayyappaswami resided. As we stepped slowly ever closer to him, my nostrils filled with the scent of jasmine, sandalwood, rosewater, charred coconut and sweat. Looking out into the gullies and ravines outside the built platform where the temple complex stood, I could see wild boars and foxes going through the trash heaps filled with the leftovers from meals, pooja ingredients and other paraphernalia.

The *darshanam* itself was a busy, almost fleeting affair in the end. I had to crane my neck really hard, pressed on all sides by sweaty writhing bodies calling out to the lord as I tried to gaze adoringly at the majesty of the young god seated in his yogic posture inside the oil-lamplit sanctum sanctorum, and after only perhaps a few moments was shoved quickly aside by the ever greedy mass of swamis yearning for their own time with the lord they had worked so hard to come pay tribute to. Then off we went to the other shrines in the complex, collecting the *prasadam* offered by the priests and cracking coconuts in the great pit set aside for the same purpose and munching on the pieces that flew back at us. We also had to take in what was called the *Bhasmakkulam*, a ritual tank with holy ash in it from countless ceremonies. After it was all done, we retired to a thatched shack with planks of coconut palm wood strapped together to form berths to sleep on. The dinner that night was also something I remember quite vividly because it was so unusual and ridiculous. Since only vegetarian fare was available at the premises, and it was quite late in the night by the time we could get around to looking for something to eat, we had to settle for porotta and sambar, which is as weird a combination to a regular malayali kid as pancakes and hot sauce to some of my Canadian friends.

Porotta, the flaky all-purpose flour flatbreads, were usually p[aired with savoury non-vegetarian delicacies like egg roast, chicken, beef or pork while Sambar was the chaste vegetable curry accompanying such south Indian classics as dosha and idli, typical breakfast fare across the peninsula. I found the combination to be extraordinarily odd, especially the texture and flavour, which felt like a forbidden novelty because you just don't mess around with the classics.

I visited Sabarimala several times after that, a;lweays with my father, like it was our own little boys' day out. I only ever partook in the fasting and such one other time. The rest of the time the tripos were almost always impromptu, me tagging along with my father because we had nothing else to do at home and he had been asked to accompany someone because of his connections. On these occasions, I did not climb up the special 18 steps, but instead used a side staircase reserved for the staff and policemen of the temple. I nevertheless had the privilege of standing at the very front of the queue, separated from the other devotees, right at the footstep of the *thirunada* on these latter visits, and afterwards rest on comfortable couches under cool ceiling fans in the office buildings, sometimes in the presence of high-ranking priests and officials. This was of course unorthodox and unusual, but was only possible because my father had worked at the time for someone who was connected to the family of the head priest. I haven't been back in over a decade, and it is unlikely I will be back anytime soon either, although my father has been going at least once or twice a year up until now. My mother is also now looking forward to joining in, excited to do the pilgrimage she had long agon performed with her own father. She's older now, considered a mother-figure to the ascetic, celibate and apparently rather easily distracted mountain deity.

Another pilgrimage that is a favourite of my family's, though not as often visited, was the out-of-place pair of small shrines in a place called Mankombu, near Erattupetta in Kottayam. Sitting half way up another mountain, though far more accessible now through an actual tarmac road unlike its dilapidated days from my childhood, the location has a pair of shrines dedicated to goddesses. It sits in the shadow of the majestic *Illikkkal Kallu*, a towering rocky outcrop that always reminded of Dracula's castle when viewed from the temple complex with the rising sun behind it especially. Of the two Devis residing here, one is a brahmanised goddess in an encircled traditional Malayali temple structure while the other sits on a lower level amidst the wilderness and a natural spring flowing next to it representing a Vana Durga or forest goddess, hearkening back to the pre-Aryanised worship practices of the Dravidian-speaking people. It is believed that the goddess residing here was smuggled out from the Tamil country centuries ago by my father's ancestral community of Vellala Pillais who were fleeing the wrath of a king. They brought their ancestral devi to this beautiful location and have been caring for her ever since, despite the ongoing disputes with the erstwhile royal Poonjar family. I visited this shrine earlier in 2024 when I had gone back home after five years in Canada, and it was just as peaceful and beautiful as I remembered it and the silhouette of the Kallu was ominous as ever as well. This time instead of walking up a barely maintained winding road that buses didn't ply when I was a kid we drove down the other side with my sister-in-law in tow with my six year-old nephew. Not being particularly religious myself, I nevertheless felt pleased to introduce the little guy to a little milestone from my own days as a boy growing up in Kerala.

The last place I have to mention where we went on pilgrimage a few times for a short while when I was a boy was the *sarppakkavu* or serpent-shrine of Pambummekkattu Mana near Thrissur. While not a location we visited consistently throughout my life, the circumstances leading up to a few repeat visits around the time I was eleven or twelve feel particularly curious and specifically Malayali. The shrine is dedicated to the Sarpam or serpent spirits that had been worshipped long before the

Aryanisation of the Darvidian-speaking people, powers considered older and more attuned with the natural world of the ordinary Malayali. *Sarppakavu* are attached to most Malayali temples, but usually just outside the Brahmanical enclosure in wooded or wild areas where the flora and fauna are allowed to flourish unchecked around the carved stone idols representing these ancient spirits. You could say that we didn't choose this particular pilgrimage but the spirits compelled us into it. It all started when a few of my cousins and I began having vivid and extremely realistic dreams about snakes around the same time. One of mine that I remember was one where I was about to step out into our backyard but couldn't because there were two-headed hooded cobras prancing around the place doing some kind of ritualistic dance. Another one had my parents and I returning from the cinema late at night, only to find a huge pit of snakes rolling and twisting in it blocking our path into which my mother pushed me in for some reason. They weren't very pleasant, I must admit. Even worse were the near misses with actual real-life serpents some of us had accompanying these dreams. There was the time my mother went into the old shed behind the house to collect firewood and had to jump out of the way when an angry black cobra rose up from a pile of ash and lashed out at her. Not long after that I was sitting on a pile of bricks that had been collected for the renovation work at an uncle's house. Moments after I had gotten up and started walking away, a snake slithered out from the pile and made its way into the bushes at the edge of the compound, leaving my cousin who I was talking with and I dumbfounded. After a few such instances had happened to a few of us, the elders decided that something had to be done and next thing I knew we were driving off to this temple I had never heard of before in my life. There were several trips in a relatively short period of time to this place, no doubt in an attempt to figure out the supposed cause and solution for these inauspicious incidents through divine intervention. I particularly remember the first trip there. We had driven down in the ubiquitous taxi of my childhood, the Hindustan Ambassador, that one of my father's friends owned. The old-school house which was the residence of the family adept at this particular branch of Malayali religious tradition was surrounded by dense foliage, with tall trees covered in vines and moss and the walls and other surfaces adorned with serpentine statues and motifs. Before we went in though we had to take a ceremonial dip in the big pond nearby, and walk shivering through a narrow lane with high brick walls on both sides with trees looming over us. What I remember most distinctly from that day however isn't anything particularly religious or miraculous. In the expansive grove attached to the house there were all these different types of trees that seemingly were bearing the same fruit. These fruits were also of unusual size and proportion, rather long and dangling and dark in shade at least from the distance at which I was seeing them. It puzzled me, but I put the thought away as we entered the sacred space and went on with the ceremonies. The day was failing by the time we came out. It was then that I noticed the curious dangling fruits wriggled around for a bit, and then spread their leathery wings and started to fly away. They weren't fruits, but fruit bats. Hundreds of them took wing at the same time, almost covering the whole sky with their webbed wings, off for their nightly forage. It was a truly eerie yet magnificent sight. Every time I visited the place after that I looked forward to seeing the bats, even if they were just dangling in their daily slumber. After a few pilgrimages there, the snake dreams did stop although I personally am loath to credit it to anything religious or supernatural. I haven't been back to the shrine since.

Apart from these pilgrimages that were taken often, I have had the privilege to visit other prominent centres of pilgrimage in India. Some of them are obscure while others are some of the holiest sites in Hinduism that most Hindus would give an arm and a leg to be able to visit. The closest of these to my home was a little shrine called Amaramkavu which is a sacred grove dedicated to a

Vana Durga that I visited only once as a child. It is a wild and untamed space of some three acres, the wilderness allowed to claim this space close to my hometown hearkening back to a pre-Brahmin era. The goddess here was represented in an idol place inside a shrine without a roof so that she can be bathed in the rain, the wind, the sun and the moonlight. The day I paid her a visit, it was raining cats and dogs. The rain was so torrential in fact that my parents and I were stuck at the temple for what felt like hours. The place felt primal and wild to me, but in a very appealing way. It felt like a place from a different time. Goddesses have always been my favourites from the Hindu pantheon, and I'm especially partial to the two martial goddesses Durga and Bhadrakali. Perhaps that's why this interaction spoke to me at a deep and visceral level. Or maybe it was the fact that she resided in a wild deep wood of her own unbothered by people and enjoying the downpour in peace.

Another devi I visited, but this time at great peril, was the lady residing at Mangala Devi near

Thekkady. This dilapidated shrine, a ruin from older times, is dedicated to Kannagi, the heroine of the Sangam era (300 BCE to 100 CE) Tamil classic *Chilappathikaram*. Situated in the middle of the forests near Thekkady on top of a steep hill, the shrine is inaccessible to people except for one day a year. On every *Chitra Pournami* devotees are however allowed to pay her a visit and offer obeisance under the supervision of the police as the area is claimed by both Kerala and Tamil Nadu. The way to the shrine is extremely dangerous. There is no road to speak of. The trail is rough, winding and treacherous and passable only either on foot or using sturdy 4*4 off-road vehicles with expert drivers. Besides the possibility of the vehicle breaking down or falling off the cliff into the deep ravines, the location is home to the wildlife of the reserved forests of Kerala and the possibility of waylaying such beasts as elephants, boars, bears, wild dogs, leopards, gaur (Indian wild buffalo) and even the reclusive tigers are not insignificant. I was able to make the trip because my father was working in the Periyar Tiger Reserve at the time and we could go along with a party of the department that had sturdy vehicles and drivers, not to mention nerves of steel. The whole experience, of riding up the rugged trail, the views offered by the verdant green of the Western Ghats, the cool refreshing air, the mysteries whispered by the ancient stone blocks of the ruins etc are still exhilarating and nearly unmatched.

Not nearly as dangerous but as exciting was the exhaustingly long trek up another mountain I partook as an adult when I joined my family in climbing to the hallowed mountain top shrine of Vaishnodevi in Jammu and Kashmir. Unfamiliar to most south Indians I know, this remote shrine nevertheless is as important up north as Sabarimala or Tirupathi is down south. It had been a dream destination for my mother, a deeply devout Hindu from a brahmin Namboothiri background who also spent years in north India with my father as newlyweds. For me the shrine was only significant as a location that I had seen on the television in

Hindi serials and the devotional show *Jai Mata Di* which featured it prominently. I also knew how many people would saw off their right hand for an opportunity for a pilgrimage here. So when we were visiting my brother who was stationed in Srinagar, it was inevitable that we would take advantage of the moment and fulfil this great wish of my mother's. There are three manifestations of the elemental and universal female spirit known in Hinduism as Shakthi, considered here manifestations of Vaishno Devi, represented in idols in deep recesses washed perennially by mountain springs. The trek up the mountainside was not easy, and is considered a significant part of the penance and duty of the devotee wishing to see this benevolent goddess. My company, which included my parents and sister-in-law along with myself, took the charming local mountain-route train which wound its way next to deep gorges and steep cliffs from Srinagar to the base camp of the trek. From this location there were a number of ways to reach the shrine some fifteen kilometres up the steep rocky mountainside at an elevation of about 1700 metres. The really indigent or indulgent could take a swift helicopter ride, and the rest had the choice between being carried up by a quartet of gentlemen in a rude palanquin, on horseback or plain old walking. We decided to opt for the horses. The animals available were incredibly patient and calm, trained to carry novices with no experience and probably unsteady on horseback from sheer fear or excitement. They trotted steadily up the winding, often steep path up the mountainside with minimal supervision from the person in charge of them leading at the front. I must say I felt like a king sitting atop that horse, towering over everyone around me, my long black oiled hair dancing in the wind. The views as we made the climb were nothing to laugh at. The sun was setting over the valleys below and the shadows cast by the surrounding mountains and the changing hues of sunlight from this height were truly wondrous to behold. Nearly half way up, we had to ditch the horse and carry on by foot. I still have no idea how my poor mother managed it. She had been suffering from muscle pains and circulation issues in her legs, but I guess the placebo power of devotion was strong that night because she climbed all the way up without needing no more than a few breaks. By the time we reached the summit and entered the well-organised premises, I was exhausted and it was nearly midnight, but we joined the queues and paid our respect to all three goddesses. Once the rare milestone was fulfilled, and we had rested for about half an hour on the summit, we made our way back down the mountain, an easier prospect now that we were filled with the joy of accomplishment and the call of our cosy mattresses in our hotel rooms.

Of course I have also had the good luck to visit two of the holiest pilgrimage centres from a hindu perspective; Haridwar and Varanasi. The trip to Haridwar was when I was twelve, as an extension to the Delhi-Agra-Mathura trip we were on. We stayed in rooms adjacent to a lord Ayyappa temple there operated by some Malayalis. In the day and a half we had, we visited a number of shrines song the riverbank, took the customary dip in the freezing waters of the holy Ganga and watched the renowned *aarti* at dusk when the priests lighted hundreds of oil lamps and made the whole riverside look like the galaxy from whence the mythical river is said to have been brought down to earth. It was beautiful and memorable, but none of my deeply wished prayers were answered and then I knew no one was listening. There has never been an urge to go back. The trip to Varanasi was during the aforementioned Srinagar visit, once again at my mother's insistence. The "quick" detour from Delhi took an extra twelve hours thanks to the always reliable northern train schedules. I found Varanasi to be an extreme disappointment, not only from a spiritual sense but from an aesthetic one as well as the streets were dirty and ill-kempt, litter, cow dung and pan spittle covering most of the surfaces. There didn't seem to be any civic sense among the residents of the place. The famed ghats were also filthy, and I only took the dip in the Ganga to satisfy my mothers wishes, having to take a shower the moment we returned to our rooms. As much sin of the individual can be washed away by the holy river, it seemed to me that the whole city itself needed to be cleansed. Things may have changed since, but I have no interest in going back. I was happy for my mother, and glad that I could do this pilgrimage with her, but I was glad to see the back of that eyesore and return to the rain soaked quieter environs of my south Indian ambalams.

Other pilgrimages to destinations big and small populate my life so far. Over cobbles. Sand, gravel, cement and mud I have walked in the search for god's grace or my mother's happiness. I have visited almost all the major hindu temples in Kerala, even spending four days in front of the Vadakkunnathan temple in Thrissur for a camp about Hinduism in my late teens because I was bored during the summer holidays, but these days my pilgrimages are of a different sort. People and places from history call me now. I travel to pay homage to ideas, symbols, people, buildings, things of stone and mortar. This year my pilgrimage was to the graves of two extraordinary women from the history of

India, Sultan Raziyya and Jahanara Begum. Others await their turns in the coming years, a lifetime's worth of stories and experiences to cherish. The experiences I have had were wonderful, and I remember them fondly for the most part but it's now time to lay them to rest and embark on the secular and personal stage of pilgrimages. I am seeking deeper meaning, balms to my soul and joy to my spirit but not through the lens of religion or worship, through community or obligation but through solitude, mindfulness and seeking that which educates, enlightens and invigorates beyond the realm of the supernatural. Everyone has their own pilgrimages to do, and mine for myself have only just begun. Oh what a wonderful idea it is, this vista in front of me of unnumbered destinations just for my own personal pilgrimage, by my own volition.

Acknowledgments

This book has been in the making for nearly twelve years, though that was never planned that way. I had a hard time writing anything substantial for nearly fifteen years, but there have been people all along who have provided me with inspiration and encouragement without whom any amount of writing would not have taken place. First and foremost is my mother. She encouraged my reading and writing unconditionally, even when I couldn't often find the spark within myself. I am also indebted to Dr. Aswathy Balachandran, my favourite professor from my undergraduate years. Her kind words, encouragement and effervescent spirit has always been a buoy to my spirit, apart from the delicious meals she has cooked for me over the years at the many dinners I had the pleasure of joining in with her family. She is my fairy godmother in many ways. I would also like to express my gratitude to Anurag Nair, my friend, who was instrumental in me taking care of my mental health over the course of the years the pieces in this book were written. He has read more of writing than anyone and been honest with his critiques, and that is worth its weight in gold. And finally, I must offer thanks to every one of my friends, family and colleagues over the years who have patiently listened to me talk about all the ideas I have had that wanted to write about, all the frustrations I have vented at them and all the topics I have exhausted their patience with because of my enthusiasm.

About the Author

Arjun currently lives in Kapuskasing, a small town in northern Ontario where he spends his free time swimming in the lakes, cooking recipes borrowed from his mother and reading as many books as he can get his hands on about history. He is a former student of Mar Athanasius College in Kothamangalam and Cambrian College in Sudbury with postgraduate credentials in English and HR Management. This is his first book to be published.

www.ingramcontent.com/pod-product-compliance
Lightning Source LLC
Chambersburg PA
CBHW030337310726
48979CB00001B/71